15/-

POEMS FOR PLEASURE

BOOK III
Commentary

POEMS FOR PLEASURE

CHOSEN AND EDITED BY

A. F. SCOTT

BOOK III

COMMENTARY
(METHOD OF TEACHING SELECTED POEMS)

SECOND EDITION
WITH AN APPENDIX
(EXPOSITION OF SELECTED POEMS)

CAMBRIDGE
AT THE UNIVERSITY PRESS
1957

PUBLISHED BY
THE SYNDICS OF THE CAMBRIDGE UNIVERSITY PRESS

Bentley House, 200 Euston Road, London, N.W. 1
American Branch: 32 East 57th Street, New York 22, N.Y.

First Edition 1955
Second Edition 1957

Printed in Great Britain at the University Press, Cambridge
(Brooke Crutchley, University Printer)

CONTENTS

Preface to the Second Edition   *page* xiii

Introduction   xv

COMMENTARY: METHOD

PART I

§1. RHYTHM IN VERSE

Sail Hauling	TRADITIONAL	3
Widdicombe Fair	TRADITIONAL	3
Off the Ground	WALTER DE LA MARE	4
The Owl and the Pussy Cat	EDWARD LEAR	5
The Pobble who has no Toes	EDWARD LEAR	6
The Jumblies	EDWARD LEAR	6
The Dong with a Luminous Nose	EDWARD LEAR	7
The Akond of Swat	EDWARD LEAR	8

§2. PICTURES IN WORDS

The Eagle	LORD TENNYSON	9
The Eagle	ANDREW YOUNG	10
Silver	WALTER DE LA MARE	10
The Poor Man's Pig	EDMUND BLUNDEN	11
Milk for the Cat	HAROLD MONRO	12
Winter	WILLIAM SHAKESPEARE	13
Miss Thompson goes Shopping	MARTIN ARMSTRONG	14

§3. TALES AND MINSTRELSY

Green Broom	TRADITIONAL	15
The Fox jumped up on a Moonlight Night	TRADITIONAL	15

CONTENTS

The Frolicsome Duke   TRADITIONAL   *page* 16
The Pied Piper of Hamelin   ROBERT BROWNING   17
The Jackdaw of Rheims   R. H. BARHAM   26

§4. THE POET'S FEELING

The Fiddler of Dooney   W. B. YEATS   28
To the Cuckoo   WILLIAM WORDSWORTH   29
The Darkling Thrush   THOMAS HARDY   30
An Old Woman of the Roads   PADRAIC COLUM   31
The Lamb   WILLIAM BLAKE   31
The Tyger   WILLIAM BLAKE   32
The Bells of Heaven   RALPH HODGSON   34

PART II
§1. THE POET'S SONG

Come unto these Yellow Sands   WILLIAM SHAKESPEARE   37
The Echoing Green   WILLIAM BLAKE   38
Blow, Blow, thou Winter
     Wind   WILLIAM SHAKESPEARE   40
Now the Hungry Lion Roars   WILLIAM SHAKESPEARE   41
Overheard on a Saltmarsh   HAROLD MONRO   42
Full Fathom Five   WILLIAM SHAKESPEARE   43

§2. THE NATURAL SCENE

Spring   THOMAS NASHE   45
Home-Thoughts, from Abroad   ROBERT BROWNING   46
The Daffodils   WILLIAM WORDSWORTH   47
Pied Beauty   GERARD MANLEY HOPKINS   49
Inversnaid   GERARD MANLEY HOPKINS   50
The Thrush's Nest   JOHN CLARE   51
The Pike   EDMUND BLUNDEN   52

CONTENTS

§3. BALLADS OLD AND NEW

Sir Patrick Spens	TRADITIONAL	*page* 54
The Wife of Usher's Well	TRADITIONAL	56
The Twa Corbies	TRADITIONAL	58
Lord Randal	TRADITIONAL	60
Heriot's Ford	RUDYARD KIPLING	61
O What is that Sound	W. H. AUDEN	62

§4. THE POET'S HEART

Upon Westminster Bridge	WILLIAM WORDSWORTH	64
Jerusalem	WILLIAM BLAKE	65
There was an Indian	J. C. SQUIRE	66
On first looking into Chapman's Homer	JOHN KEATS	67

PART III

§1. THE MAGIC OF WORDS

Romance	W. J. TURNER	73
Epilogue to 'Hassan'	JAMES ELROY FLECKER	74
Cargoes	JOHN MASEFIELD	75
Lepanto	G. K. CHESTERTON	76
Tarantella	HILAIRE BELLOC	78

§2. THE POET'S VISION

To Autumn	JOHN KEATS	80
Ode to the West Wind	P. B. SHELLEY	83
The Cloud	P. B. SHELLEY	85
The Ice-Cart	W. W. GIBSON	86

Winter the Huntsman   OSBERT SITWELL   *page* 88
London Snow   ROBERT BRIDGES   89
Snow in the Suburbs   THOMAS HARDY   91

§3. NARRATIVE POEMS ON SEA AND LAND

High Tide on the Coast of
    Lincolnshire, 1571   JEAN INGELOW   93
The 'Revenge'   LORD TENNYSON   95
The Destruction of
    Sennacherib   LORD BYRON   98
The Battle of the Baltic   THOMAS CAMPBELL   99
The Burial of Sir John Moore   CHARLES WOLFE   101
The Cavalier's Escape   WALTER THORNBURY   102
How they brought the Good
    News from Ghent to Aix   ROBERT BROWNING   105

§4. THE POET AND THE MODERN WORLD

The Secret of the Machines   RUDYARD KIPLING   107
The Pigeon   RICHARD CHURCH   108
Prelude   T. S. ELIOT   109
To Iron-Founders and Others   GORDON BOTTOMLEY   110

PART IV
§1. THE MUSIC OF POETRY

Hymn to Diana   BEN JONSON   113
Song for St Cecilia's Day   JOHN DRYDEN   114
The Reaper   WILLIAM WORDSWORTH   116
Blow, Bugle, Blow   LORD TENNYSON   117
The Lotos Eaters   LORD TENNYSON   118
L'Allegro   JOHN MILTON   120

§2. SCENES OF THE MACHINE AGE

Morning Express	SIEGFRIED SASSOON	*page* 122
The Bridge	JOHN REDWOOD ANDERSON	123
The Express	STEPHEN SPENDER	125
Night Mail	W. H. AUDEN	126

§3. STORIES OF PURE IMAGINATION

The Dirge of Lovely Rosabelle	SIR WALTER SCOTT	128
La Belle Dame Sans Merci	JOHN KEATS	130
Kubla Khan	SAMUEL TAYLOR COLERIDGE	131
The Listeners	WALTER DE LA MARE	132
Flannan Isle	W. W. GIBSON	134

§4. THE ETERNAL THEME

Integer Vitae	THOMAS CAMPION	136
To Daffodils	ROBERT HERRICK	137
Virtue	GEORGE HERBERT	138
A Slumber did my Spirit Seal	WILLIAM WORDSWORTH	140
Prospice	ROBERT BROWNING	142
Up-hill	CHRISTINA ROSSETTI	143
Fidele	WILLIAM SHAKESPEARE	145

APPENDIX: EXPOSITION

BOOK I

Daniel	VACHEL LINDSAY	147
The Congo	VACHEL LINDSAY	148
Weathers	THOMAS HARDY	150
Robin Hood and Little John	TRADITIONAL	150
The Rainbow	WILLIAM WORDSWORTH	151
A Birthday	CHRISTINA ROSSETTI	152
To the Cuckoo	WILLIAM WORDSWORTH	152

CONTENTS

The Darkling Thrush	THOMAS HARDY	*page* 153
The Vagabond	ROBERT LOUIS STEVENSON	153
The Woodlark	GERARD MANLEY HOPKINS	154
Return of Spring	LORD TENNYSON	155
The Kingfisher	W. H. DAVIES	156
The Hollow Wood	EDWARD THOMAS	156
The Flycatcher	SYLVIA LYND	157
Mallard	REX WARNER	158
Lapwing	REX WARNER	159
Bat	D. H. LAWRENCE	160
Snake	D. H. LAWRENCE	161
Horses on the Camargue	ROY CAMPBELL	161
Helen of Kirconnell	TRADITIONAL	162
Jock of Hazeldean	SIR WALTER SCOTT	162
Lochinvar	SIR WALTER SCOTT	163
Lord Ullin's Daughter	THOMAS CAMPBELL	163
Henry Hudson's Voyage	DOROTHY WELLESLEY	164
You That Love England	C. DAY LEWIS	164
How Sleep the Brave	WILLIAM COLLINS	166
Men of England	THOMAS CAMPBELL	166
It is not to be thought of that the Flood	WILLIAM WORDSWORTH	167
Bermudas	ANDREW MARVELL	167
Ulysses	LORD TENNYSON	168

BOOK II

Romance	W. J. TURNER	171
Eldorado	EDGAR ALLAN POE	171
Portrait of a Boy	STEPHEN VINCENT BENET	171
Lepanto	G. K. CHESTERTON	172
Rio Grande	SACHEVERELL SITWELL	176

CONTENTS

On the Coast of Coromandel	OSBERT SITWELL	*page* 177
Now the Full-throated Daffodils	C. DAY LEWIS	177
Ode to Evening	WILLIAM COLLINS	179
Poem in October	DYLAN THOMAS	181
The Old Ships	JAMES ELROY FLECKER	184
The Spanish Armada	LORD MACAULAY	184
The Loss of the 'Royal George'	WILLIAM COWPER	187
The War Song of Dinas Vawr	T. L. PEACOCK	188
The Ballad of Agincourt	MICHAEL DRAYTON	188
1805	ROBERT GRAVES	190
Hohenlinden	THOMAS CAMPBELL	191
Waterloo	LORD BYRON	192
After Blenheim	ROBERT SOUTHEY	193
Hart-leap Well	WILLIAM WORDSWORTH	193
The Colubriad	WILLIAM COWPER	194
The Pigeon	RICHARD CHURCH	195
To a Telegraph Pole	LOUIS UNTERMEYER	195
Factory Windows	VACHEL LINDSAY	196
He will watch the Hawk	STEPHEN SPENDER	196
To Iron-Founders and Others	GORDON BOTTOMLEY	197
To Some Builders of Cities	STANLEY SNAITH	199
Beleaguered Cities	F. L. LUCAS	199
Clock	HAROLD MONRO	199
Matin Song	THOMAS HEYWOOD	200
At the Round Earth's Imagined Corners	JOHN DONNE	201
Sweet Musick	JOHN FLETCHER	201
The Lotos-Eaters: Choric Song	LORD TENNYSON	201
L'Allegro	JOHN MILTON	203

xi

CONTENTS

The Landscape near an Aerodrome	STEPHEN SPENDER	*page* 210
The Pylons	STEPHEN SPENDER	211
Crucifixion of the Skyscraper	J. GOULD FLETCHER	212
The Lady of Shalott	LORD TENNYSON	212
The Blessèd Damozel	DANTE GABRIEL ROSSETTI	213
Eve	RALPH HODGSON	216
Goblin Market	CHRISTINA ROSSETTI	216
The Forsaken Merman	MATTHEW ARNOLD	217
Outlaws	ROBERT GRAVES	218
The Perfect Life	BEN JONSON	219
Sweet Content	THOMAS DEKKER	219
The Character of a Happy Life	SIR HENRY WOTTON	220
Integer Vitae	THOMAS CAMPION	221
Death the Leveller	JAMES SHIRLEY	221
Virtue	GEORGE HERBERT	222
On the Tombs in Westminster Abbey	FRANCIS BEAUMONT	222
Elegy Written in a Country Churchyard	THOMAS GRAY	223
Patch-Shaneen	J. M. SYNGE	227
Prognosis	LOUIS MACNEICE	228
The Chariot	EMILY DICKINSON	229
Peace	HENRY VAUGHAN	229
And Death Shall Have No Dominion	DYLAN THOMAS	229
Book List		232

xii

PREFACE TO THE SECOND EDITION

This commentary was originally designed to put forward a number of different ways of presenting poetry in secondary schools.

It has now been suggested that the usefulness of the book might be increased if a further commentary were added, concerned solely with the explanation of difficulties in the poems in the anthology (including some poems already touched on).

This edition contains such a commentary as an appendix. It will be seen that the notes are on several different levels: some throw light on the poem by giving the story, legend or incident on which it is based; others try to explain the image or symbol which gives significance to the poem; some seek to elucidate allusions, references and other factual material; or to explain obscurities in grammar and syntax; others give a detailed paraphrase. The main concern throughout is to try to help as far as possible towards a full understanding of the poem. No critical assessment of the poetry is attempted.

It is not, of course, intended that all this material should be used in the class-room. How far one should give detailed explanation of poetry to a class is a matter best left to the discretion of the teacher. The 'experience' of the poem as spoken or read may well be enough. The individual teacher, however, should understand, as fully as possible, the meaning of the poem being presented, to enable him both to read the poem as it should be read, and to give whatever explanation he may consider necessary. I hope this commentary may help in that respect.

A.F.S.

3 April 1957

INTRODUCTION

Coleridge once said, 'In order to obtain adequate notions of any truth we must intellectually separate its distinguishable parts; and this is the technical process of philosophy'. We would separate its distinguishable parts to gain a greater understanding of those elements before reconsidering the subject as a whole. Might this not also be a way of approaching poetry?

When we consider the 'distinguishable parts' of poetry we see that a poem consists of a tune, a picture, a story and a feeling. These are, of course, closely related, fused into a single artistic whole, yet it should be possible to consider each part singly. Furthermore, one can select poems which will show each distinguishable part above the rest. This would serve as an introduction to the range and scope of poetry and lead perhaps more effectively to a fuller appreciation.

What part should be considered first when presenting poetry to children? The most rewarding approach is through the music of words. Begin with the words, for as Mallarmé says, 'Poetry is not made with ideas, but is made of words'.

Begin more simply with the sound of the single word. Arouse interest in the sound by asking what words would best describe the knock on the door, the noise of a train, the sound of the sea? Get the class to recognize the variety of the sound of words: the whispering, soothing, quiet words; the loud, sonorous, roaring words. Add to the effect by placing words together: *lively din, sullen roar, flickering lightning, thunder clap.*

Here one should try to gain recognition of the sound before the sense, the sound above the sense. Read passages of poetry where the sound predominates and the class will respond to the sound. From pairs of words we pass to groups of words, again with sound predominating:

The murmurous haunt of flies on summer eves.

Now the sound will have movement:

The poplars' noise of falling showers.

The heavy and light words will begin to weave their own pattern and a tune will begin to emerge. A tune like the multitude of sounds used to reproduce the music of water, in calm:

lapping on the crag
And the long ripple washing in the reeds.

or in storm:

To roar rock-thwarted under bellowing caves.

Let the tune be the source of enjoyment, not the meaning. Why bother about meaning now? We are striving to draw on the child's instinctive love of tune. Children enjoy listening to the music of poetry not only in their own language but also in an unknown tongue. They have an intuitive insight into the meaning of mere sound. We should remember that long before articulate speech existed emotion was expressed and communicated in sound. It still is so communicated apart from the mere dictionary meaning of the words used. A proper feeling for words is the right beginning for the enjoyment of poetry.

If we make the appeal through the sound, then nursery rhymes, traditional tales, nonsense verse will all exemplify the tune. The verse will march and slide and dance along. Children should be encouraged to recognize the different tunes; to be able to say whether the verse is cheerful or sad, gay or melancholy; whether it indicates delight or a sense of loss. There is no need to consider metrical structure at this point, but to distinguish the tune, to be aware of the pace at which the given line should move, and to recognize the proper way in which a poem should be read:

When Ajax strives some rock's vast weight to throw,
The line too labours, and the words move slow;
Not so, when swift Camilla scours the plain,
Flies o'er th' unbending corn, and skims along the main.

Sound adds another pleasure to the ear in the form of rhyme.
Children enjoy this repetition of like sounds which sets up its own
tide of expectations, and can produce a lulling and hypnotic effect
as in:

We are the music-makers,
And we are the dreamers of dreams,
Wandering by lone sea-breakers,
And sitting by desolate streams;
World-losers and world-forsakers,
On whom the pale moon gleams:
Yet we are the movers and shakers
Of the world for ever, it seems.

or by a different use, a liveliness and humour:

Then up with your cup: till you stagger in speech,
And match me this catch: though you swagger and screech,
And drink till you wink: my merry men each.

Further enjoyment comes with an understanding of the general
correspondence between sound and mood; when bright, lively words
are chosen for a cheerful occasion; quiet, muted words are made to
speak of peacefulness or sadness; and clashing sounds are used to
portray conflict and adventure.

We feel the peacefulness of:

Music that gentlier on the spirit lies,
Than tired eyelids upon tired eyes;
Music that brings sweet sleep down from the blissful skies.

(an effect produced by the consummate skill in using that *s*) and the
harsh vigour of:

Dry clash'd his harness in the icy caves
And barren chasms, and all to left and right
The bare black cliff clang'd round him, as he based
His feet on juts of slippery crag that rang
Sharp-smitten with the dint of armèd heels—
And on a sudden, lo! the level lake,
And the long glories of the winter moon.

(with the strong contrast provided by the soft liquid sound of the last two lines). There is no need to explain. These effects can be felt:

> There is not wind enough to twirl
> The one red leaf, the last of its clan,
> That dances as often as dance it can,
> Hanging so light, and hanging so high,
> On the topmost twig that looks up at the sky.

Here the tune suggests what the words describe.

Humpty Dumpty said that he made words mean exactly what he wanted them to mean, and poets through the generations have given a particular flavour, a richness of association to many words; words such as *golden, royal, rose, star, faery, magic, dawn*. And these, the 'chosen coin of fancy', flash out from many a golden phrase that has

> Charm'd magic casements, opening on the foam
> Of perilous seas, in faery lands forlorn.

or told of:

> Old, unhappy, far-off things,
> And battles long ago.

Not only are ordinary words enriched in sound and in special association, but poets draw upon the whole realm of proper names, words already opulent in sound and in romantic association, and write a catalogue as sweet as this:

> whose names
> Are five sweet symphonies,
> Cecily, Gertrude, Magdalen,
> Margaret and Rosalys.

or as exotic as this:

> Not Babylon
> Nor great Alcairo such magnificence
> Equalled in all their glories, to enshrine
> Belus or Serapis their gods, or seat
> Their kings, when Egypt with Assyria strove
> In wealth and luxury.

Many poetical words recall the ceremonial origin of poetry. Dancing was probably the earliest of the arts—particularly that

xviii

ceremonial dance to placate the gods which was the beginning of religion—and when words were added to the dance it was necessary for them to be rhythmical and measured in sound so that they too would fit the elaborate ceremonial. So a number of words became the ceremonial words, and from these early poetry was composed.

Something of this ceremonial character remains in poetry, not so much in the words themselves as in the way they are used, for it is true to say that even when using the commonest words poetry does not use them commonly. This further impresses upon us that poetry by its nature and origin should be read aloud; and how important that reading is!

Poets themselves have often shown us how their poetry should be read. We think of Wordsworth with his 'terrible girt deep voice' declaiming by the rock in the path under Rydal, 'muttering and thundering of a still evening'. And Tennyson, dark and shaggy, with his booming bass voice, intoning and chanting his own poems, 'mouthing out his hollow oes and aes'.

Such declamation would be arresting and impressive. One of the commonest failings is to read poetry so quickly that the full value of the sound of the words, the rhythm of the line, and the tune of the whole are lost.

It is apparent therefore that the reading of poetry demands careful preparation. As William Empson has said, 'The process of getting to understand a poet is precisely that of constructing his poem in one's own mind'. To lead children to 'appreciate' is not merely to lead them to admire a poem but to make them become in a sense its re-creators. This is why reading a poem aloud to them is so important. And to read well one must understand the poem, must be able to bring out its music, must study not to come between the poem and its audience, recalling Hamlet's warning:

Nor do not saw the air too much with your hand, thus, but use all gently....Be not too tame neither, but let your own discretion be your tutor: suit the action to the word, the word to the action; with this special observance, that you o'erstep not the modesty of nature.

Whenever we look at a poem on the page we are at once conscious of its physical form. Compare, for example, this poem with its long, flowing line:

> For a day and a night Love sang to us, played with us,
> Folded us round from the dark and the light;
> And our hearts were fulfilled of the music he made with us,
> Made with our hearts and our lips while he stayed with us,
> Stayed in mid-passage his pinions from flight
> For a day and a night.

with this poem:

> What needs complaints,
> When she a place
> Has with the race
> Of saints?
>
> In endless mirth
> She thinks not on
> What's said or done
> In Earth.

It is valuable to examine the structure of verse because there is a definite sense in which literature is form. We recognize the significance of form in the work of the potter when he converts a lump of wet clay into a vase. We commonly admire the shape of the vase and not the substance out of which it is made, though shape and substance are one. It is somewhat similar with poetry. When the poet has cast his thought into the physical form of a sonnet or an ode we are aware that this 'shape' has given a greater significance to the theme.

The study of metrical form includes that of scansion. English verse rhythm depends upon the arrangement of stresses; stressed syllables being those we give more emphasis in natural speech. We should scan this line as follows:

$$\breve{\text{The}} \; \acute{\text{cur}} \mid \breve{\text{few}} \; \acute{\text{tolls}} \mid \breve{\text{the}} \; \acute{\text{knell}} \mid \breve{\text{of}} \; \acute{\text{part}} \mid \breve{\text{ing}} \; \acute{\text{day}} \mid$$

indicating the stressed and unstressed syllables as shown. With two syllables (the first unstressed, the second stressed) in each foot, and

five feet in the line, we recognize the verse pattern as iambic penta-
meter. Other verse patterns are the trochaic, and, with three syllable
feet, anapaestic and dactyllic. These, with the occasional feet (the
spondee, and the pyrrhic), provide the possibility of infinite variety.
In scansion, a syllable is either stressed or unstressed. This does not
take into account the varying weight of the words, from the merest
breath of sound to the heaviest weight that a word can carry. So that
along with (as it were) the basic pattern, or rhythmic norm, there is
the emphasis of the sense (open to different interpretations), and the
infinite variety of weight of words. *Lump* is a heavier word than *sun*,
both contain the *u* sound, both would take a stress in a line. These
lines from Coleridge show the difference of weight, though scansion
can show stressed and unstressed syllables only:

> With heavy thump, a lifeless lump,
> They dropped down one by one

and

> The Sun's rim dips; the stars rush out:
> At one stride comes the dark.

The poet has an instinctive ear for language and he is weighing
and measuring words habitually so as to give continuous verbal
music to his verse. Compare the following versions of *Oenone* to see
how Tennyson has improved the delicate management of vowels and
consonants:

> There is a dale in Ida, lovelier
> Than any in old Ionia, beautiful
> With emerald slopes of sunny sward, that lean
> Above the loud glenriver, which hath worn
> A path thro' steepdown granite walls below
> Mantled with flowering tendriltwine

and:

> There lies a vale in Ida, lovelier
> Than all the valleys of Ionian hills.
> The swimming vapour slopes athwart the glen,
> Puts forth an arm, and creeps from pine to pine,
> And loiters, slowly drawn.

Here, as in all poetry, we notice the importance of the order of the words. The sedate, melancholy movement of Collins' *Ode to Evening* depends as much on the arrangement as on the careful choice of words. The poet often so places the words that they must be spoken separately, avoiding the slur or elision common in everyday speech. To have written 'as he oft rises' in the line:

> As oft he rises 'midst the twilight path

would have led to the possible slurring of the words 'he' and 'oft'. The tone of a poem (the manner of reading compelled upon one) is further set by delicate artistry in the use of assonance, alliteration, internal echoes, as shown in this stanza with its cadence and dying fall:

> And hamlets brown, and dim-discover'd spires,
> And hears their simple bell, and marks o'er all
> Thy dewy fingers draw
> The gradual dusky veil.

Now we must consider in more detail the important subject of rhythm in poetry. There is the rhythm achieved by the ordinary arrangement of stressed and unstressed syllables, producing something more or less mechanical, such as:

> I sprang to the stirrup, and Joris, and he;
> I galloped, Dirck galloped, we galloped all three;
> 'Good speed!' cried the watch, as the gate-bolts undrew;
> 'Speed!' echoed the wall to us galloping through;
> Behind shut the postern, the lights sank to rest,
> And into the midnight we galloped abreast.

The consonants contribute a good deal to the metallic briskness of the passage. But it is obvious that the rhythm is, as it were, external and made to fit a selected pattern. In more complex poetry the rhythm is organic, and is part of the process of creating the poem. The poet who has been deeply moved is now translating the experience into an artistic form through the medium of words. These words will give substance to his thought and feelings, and to the images which give the emotional colouring to those thoughts and feelings. Though the poet may be shaping the poem to conform to some established verse pattern, he will also make the words conform to the flow of his feelings. Obviously a sad experience will be expressed in a poem with solemn sounds, but the poet will get closer to the actual experience than that. The rhythm of the line will follow the very rhythm of his own feelings, an organic rhythm will be created, and as this is individual the poem will not repeat the exact rhythm of a fixed metre, but have the individual mark of the poet upon it. This is the touchstone of true poetry. It can be recognized by the rhythm which will be authentic, not imposed from the outside, but created by the inner compelling rhythm of the poet's experience.

Keats, overcome by sorrow because of the death of his brother Tom, the hopelessness of his love for Fanny Brawne, the fear that he might never be a great poet, the painful realization that he too had consumption, was moved to write when he heard a nightingale singing in a Hampstead garden. The poem is not about a nightingale, but the poet's state of mind; thinking about life and death, torn by opposing feelings, Keats says:

> My heart aches, and a drowsy numbness pains
> My sense, as though of hemlock I had drunk,
> Or emptied some dull opiate to the drains
> One minute past, and Lethe-wards had sunk.

We have the heavy drugged movement of the verse down to the word 'sunk' expressing the poet's deep despondency. Then comes a shift of mood; he thinks of the song of the bird, recalling the wonder of life, and the movement of the verse, following the flow of the poet's feelings, changes:

> 'Tis not through envy of thy happy lot,
>   But being too happy in thine happiness,—
>   That thou, light-wingèd Dryad of the trees,
>   In some melodious plot
> Of beechen green, and shadows numberless,
> Singest of summer in full-throated ease.

The repetition of the word 'happy' and the use of the light-sounding words, 'envy', 'light-wingèd', 'singest', 'ease' all help to give the strongly contrasted change of rhythm: a rhythm which is as complex as the state of mind it presents.

Complexity of rhythm is shown in the following lines from Hopkins' poem *The Leaden Echo*:

> How to kéep—is there ány any, is there none such, nowhere known some, bow or brooch or braid or brace, láce, latch or catch or key to keep
> Back beauty, keep it, beauty, beauty, beauty,...from vanishing away?
> Ó is there no frowning of these wrinkles, rankèd wrinkles deep,
> Dówn? no waving off of these most mournful messengers, still messengers, sad and stealing messengers of grey?

A comparison with this 'improved' version by T. Sturge Moore shows the difference between the organic rhythm of the poet, and the mechanical rhythm of the verse-writer:

> How keep beauty? is there any way?
> Is there nowhere any means to have it stay?
> Will no bow or brooch or braid,
> Brace or lace
> Latch or catch
> Or key to lock the door lend aid
> Before beauty vanishes away?

This is, perhaps, beyond children, but the presentation of poetry to them should move towards it, from a feeling for the sound of words and the movement of verse to an appreciation of the complex rhythms of great poetry. By getting them to like some poetry we may get them ultimately to enjoy the best; not merely the attractive jingle of:

> The Assyrian came down like the wolf on the fold,
> And his cohorts were gleaming in purple and gold;
> And the sheen of their spears was like stars on the sea,
> When the blue wave rolls nightly on deep Galilee.

but also the magic of:

> Fear no more the heat o' the sun,
> Nor the furious winter's rages;

Thou thy worldly task hast done,
  Home art gone and ta'en thy wages:
Golden lads and girls all must,
As chimney-sweepers, come to dust.

Another distinguishable part of a poem is imagery. Not only is the poet a maker of verbal music, he is also a maker of pictures in words. He does not here present the symbol of a thing, but he describes and makes us see and hear the thing itself. For example, Shakespeare is not content to say that it is winter, the word 'winter' standing as the symbol of the season, but he writes:

When icicles hang by the wall,
  And Dick the shepherd blows his nail,
And Tom bears logs into the hall,
  And milk comes frozen home in pail,
When blood is nipp'd, and ways be foul,
Then nightly sings the staring owl,
                         To-whit!
To-who!—a merry note,
While greasy Joan doth keel the pot.

Here we see typical sights of winter; we feel the cold, we hear the sounds of winter itself; in fact, we experience the physical sensations of winter through the power of our imagination, which is fed by the pictures that Shakespeare gives us. Through the imagination we step into another world and see and hear things more clearly sometimes than in the real world which the poet portrays.

Some children when they cannot understand a poem ask why the poet does not express himself simply in prose. The answer is that a poet can only say what he wants to say in verse. He may be moved not merely to say that he is happy but to make us share his happiness. To do this he uses language which is heightened and enriched. Christina Rossetti expresses her happiness in these words:

My heart is like a singing-bird
  Whose nest is in a water'd shoot;
My heart is like an apple-tree
  Whose boughs are bent with thick-set fruit;

> My heart is like a rainbow shell
> That paddles in a halcyon sea;
> My heart is gladder than all these,
> Because my love is come to me.

Here, a series of similes gives us a series of pictures, each one concentrated in a way that is typical of poetry. Simile and metaphor are truly poetic, they bring together disparate objects in a way which illuminates each. The poet is always finding the similarity in dissimilars and expressing his exciting discoveries in the universe around him. The pictures the poet creates through the powers of the imagination are often more vivid than the things we see ourselves; the poet lives, as it were, at the tip of his sensations.

Tennyson portrays an eagle unforgettably in this poem:

> He clasps the crag with crooked hands;
> Close to the sun in lonely lands,
> Ringed with the azure world, he stands.
>
> The wrinkled sea beneath him crawls;
> He watches from his mountain-walls,
> And like a thunderbolt he falls.

We identify ourselves with the eagle and join it on the high crag. To describe the sea far beneath, the poet might have used such words as 'distant', 'far-off'; with masterly concentration he fixes the image with the two words, 'wrinkled' and 'crawls'—words that are so effective we feel dizzy from the sense of height.

Poetry is full of such pictures, and we should stimulate the imagination of children by considering carefully not only the pictorial images but also those appealing to the other senses. We should ask why certain words have been used, what their effect is, how the picture should be drawn, how the line should be read. At the same time we should bear in mind that imagery is not mere decoration, that it is not something added but is the very material of poetry itself.

Another pleasure in the pictorial quality of poetry is that of recognition. We often find that a poet's imagery fills out and completes our own partial knowledge of things by that flash of recognition which both instructs and delights; familiar objects are revealed in a new light, and the unfamiliar suddenly becomes real.

No one can read *The Ancient Mariner* without realizing its imaginative power:

> All in a hot and copper sky
> The bloody Sun, at noon,
> Right up above the mast did stand,
> No bigger than the Moon.

Here we are conscious not only of the colour and of the oppressive heat, but also of a stifling sensation. Imagery of this kind can stimulate all our sense impressions. In this passage:

> St Agnes' Eve—Ah, bitter chill it was!
> The owl, for all his feathers, was a-cold;
> The hare limp'd trembling through the frozen grass
> And silent was the flock in woolly fold.

so vivid is the picture in the third line with those two words 'limp'd' and 'trembling' that we seem to take part in the very sensations of the hare. Without such imagery poetry might easily become abstract; instead we have that poetic skill which gives to airy nothings 'a local habitation and a name'.

It has been truly said that 'perceptive experience is the ultimate source of almost all if not quite all of our imaginative life'; we must try to preserve this perceptive sensitiveness in children, for imagery is the most obvious contact with the world about us. It is the poet's impression of the quality of things—of colour, shape, sound, smell, texture, taste, and by appreciating these, our response to the material world is enriched.

So far we have laid the emphasis as, I think, it should be laid upon the musical qualities and the descriptive qualities of poetry. This is the right beginning, for, of course, we do not go to poetry for information. A poem is not important for what it says but for what it *is*, just as we commonly admire a vase for its shape and colour and not for its substance. Blake writes of a sunflower thus:

> Ah, Sunflower! weary of time,
> Who countest the steps of the sun;
> Seeking after that sweet golden clime
> Where the traveller's journey is done.

whereas an encyclopaedia describes a sunflower in these words:

The common sunflower, *Helianthus annuus*, is an annual herb with a rough hairy stem, three to fifteen feet high, broad coarsely toothed rough leaves, three to twelve inches long, and heads of flowers three to six inches wide, and often one foot or more in cultivated specimens.

Naturally, we pay more attention to what is said in narrative poetry. And there is a place for the story, that distinguishable part of a poem which can be put into prose.

In early days, the wandering poet, or scôp, was the story-teller, and the stories, preserved as ballads and traditional tales, may still be admired for their simplicity and directness.

Wherever possible we should allow the poem to speak for itself. So far as the longer poems are concerned, it is dangerous when a poem such as Tennyson's *Revenge* becomes the material for a history lesson, or Jean Ingelow's *High Tide on the Coast of Lincolnshire* a geography lesson, or the *Pied Piper* a lesson in nature study.

Sometimes it is necessary to explain some of the more obscure incidents of such a poem as Scott's *Rosabelle*, perhaps by a simple paraphrase, but one must be careful not to interfere with the poetical experience. There is also the question of difficult words, complicated grammatical construction, and it is perhaps wisest to clear these points out of the way by explanation in an earlier lesson, so that when the poem comes to be read there will be no interruption for explanation or elucidation.

Lastly, we come to the fourth distinguishable part in poetry, that of feeling. Children should be able to appreciate feelings such as those of joy and longing, pity and sadness, particularly in those poems where such feelings are simply expressed. Other feelings such as those of loyalty, patriotism, love of freedom can be both stimulated and appealed to by the careful choice of poem. The feeling expressed in a poem will, of course, be emphasized by the way in which the poem is read. Here it is well not to over-simplify but to get a natural and spontaneous response from the class by asking them to suggest, after careful consideration, the way in which a given poem should be read. Such co-operation leads to a more complete understanding of the feelings expressed in a poem than to state 'this is a sad poem', and then proceed to read it to the class. There are many subtleties, shades of feeling, variations of mood from line to line and verse to verse which children, once their interest has been properly aroused, will sometimes quite penetratingly reveal.

Another question to be considered is that of sincerity. Frequently the word is loosely used, and a class may say, 'We like this poem because the poet is sincere'. Now it is not always easy to explain just what sincerity is. In the most deeply sincere poetry the words somehow produce overtones of emotion in the sensitive reader which cannot be analysed or explained. One may, however, compare two poems such as Milton's sonnet *On his Blindness* and Colley Cibber's *The Blind Boy* to show sincerity.

It is only by a slow training of taste that one grows to appreciate the finest lyrical poetry on some of the eternal themes. In such training one should beware of sentimentality, the too-ready reaction to emotion, for we are surrounded by various forms of stimulation which encourage an immediate response to a situation unworthy of that emotional reaction. Here, of course, the cinema takes the lead. There is something extremely valuable in the slow generation of pity and terror in a Shakespearean tragedy, or in a long epic poem. When we find that we are moved by so-called tragic situations which are purely incidental, then the result is a weakening and dissipating of emotion. It is the *kind* of demand made upon us in considering the arts which should be the touchstone. Certain poems, such as Shelley's *Adonais*, Tennyson's *In Memoriam*, Arnold's *Thyrsis*, make us feel the deep underlying sadness of human destiny and, at the same time, enable us to experience that joy and comfort which can be gathered from a work of art however tragic the subject may be.

Our response to poetry should be balanced and controlled, for the ultimate goal is to appreciate all the elements which it contains, and to be fully aware of the unity of the whole. When reading a poem we are, in a way, living through the experience which the poet himself lived through and fixed in a memorable form. Dr Leavis has said,

'Poetry can communicate the actual quality of experience with a subtlety and precision unapproachable by any other means.' But we can only share this experience by an appreciation of the words, for it is the words which stand for all that the poet has felt, for all that has passed through his imagination. We must never move too far away from the actual words of the poem, concentrating upon them, for although poetry and prose both use words, prose uses chiefly the meaning, whereas poetry uses *all* the qualities of words. Coleridge had this in mind when, writing of poetry, he said: 'Be it observed, however, that I include in the meaning of a word not only its correspondent object but likewise all the associations which it recalls.' These associations have been likened to the ripples caused when a stone is dropped into a pool, they can spread in widening circles to the limits of the reader's mind.

Here then is an approach to poetry; an approach through its distinguishable parts: the tune, the picture, the story, the feelings, leading by true enjoyment to a fuller understanding of the whole, for as Dryden says, 'Poetry only instructs as it delights.'

A. F. SCOTT

May, 1954

ACKNOWLEDGMENT

I wish to acknowledge my indebtedness in preparing this commentary to the following: *Voice and Verse* by A. S. T. Fisher; *Poetry Speaking for Children* by M. Gullan and P. Gurrey; *Poetry and the Teacher* by T. W. Sussams; *The Poet's Window* by W. T. Cunningham and K. E. Morgan; *Poetry for You* by C. Day Lewis; and *Teaching Poetry* compiled by The Society for Teachers of English.

A. F. S.

PART I

SECTION I

RHYTHM IN VERSE

SAIL HAULING: TRADITIONAL (p. 4)

AIM. To appreciate the vigorous rhythm, and see how it fits to the movements of sail hauling.

INTRODUCTION. Read the poem through to the class bringing out the rhythm strongly as follows:

> Blów the man dówn, bullíes
> Blów the man dówn!
> Wáy, héy; blów the man dówn.
> Blów him right dówn from the tóp of his crówn!
> Gíve us a chánce to blów the man dówn.

Before reading the poem a second time, explain briefly that sailors shouted this rhyme as they were steadily hauling up the sails on the old sailing-ships. The strong beats of each line were in time with the physical movement.

CHORAL READING. The class recites the poem emphasizing the vigorous rhythm. Several members of the class may stand out in front making the movements of sail hauling to the rhythm of the verse.

WIDDICOMBE FAIR: TRADITIONAL (p. 6)

AIM. To appreciate the general liveliness and rhythmic vigour of this traditional poem.

INTRODUCTION. Read the poem with a hearty swinging rhythm, trying to differentiate the characters of the West Country people mentioned in the poem.

CHORAL READING. Divide the class, giving the parts of Tom Pearce, the man who borrowed the old mare, and his friends to the

3

best readers. Each person must speak the name in the poem and give as distinct a character as possible. The rest of the class should take the narrative lines and all join in the second and last lines of each verse.

This poem may be done several times with the characters, Tom Pearce and the rest standing out in the front, and getting as much of a West Country accent as possible into their reading.

OFF THE GROUND: WALTER DE LA MARE (p. 8)

AIM. To enter into the fun of this poem and catch its changing rhythms, 'not too fast and not too slow'.

INTRODUCTION. Read the poem to the class. This reading should be carefully prepared to try to bring out some slight differences of character between the three farmers. Read the poem a second time showing the changing rhythms and variations of pace. The poem should be read smoothly and evenly down to the line:

'As they danced through Wool.'

The next sixteen lines from:

'And Wool gone by...'

down to:

'The great green sea'

should be spoken more slowly for the three farmers seem now to 'dance in dream'. The conversation between Farmer Bates and Farmer Giles should be spoken vigorously; the lines about Farmer Turvey should be spoken quickly down to the lines:

'Sleek with their combs
Their yellow hair....'

From here to the end read more slowly of the bewilderment and 'vacant brooding' of Farmer Bates and Farmer Giles.

CHORAL READING. Single voices should take the parts of Farmer Bates and Farmer Giles. The rest of the class should read the narrative, following the variations of pace already indicated.

4

THE OWL AND THE PUSSY-CAT: EDWARD LEAR (p. 13)

AIM. To appreciate the variety in movement and in character contained in this poem.

INTRODUCTION. Read the poem to the class bringing out the easy, smooth rhythm, and paying particular attention to the silent beat at the end of lines 2, 4, 6, 11 in the first stanza:

> The Owl and the Pussy-Cat went to sea
> In a beautiful pea-green boat, ( )
> They took some honey, and plenty of money,
> Wrapped up in a five-pound note. ( )
> The Owl looked up to the stars above,
> And sang to a small guitar, ( )
> 'O lovely Pussy! O Pussy, my love,
> What a beautiful Pussy you are,
> You are,
> You are!
> What a beautiful Pussy you are!' ( )

Give the silent beat full value in the rest of the poem.

CHORAL READING. Divide the class, selecting four to play the parts of the Owl, the Pussy-Cat, the Piggy-wig and the Turkey. The Owl and the Pussy-Cat may take the opportunity for simple mime by sitting in the front of the class either on two chairs or on the floor as in an imaginary boat. The rest of the class speaks the narrative. Owl plucks an imaginary guitar to the rhythm of the lines and then speaks his lines. Pussy-Cat speaks her lines at the beginning of the second stanza. Then after the line:

> 'To the land where the Bong-tree grows'

they both get out of the boat and see Piggy-wig standing near. They walk to him and Owl speaks the first line of the third stanza and two

5

words of the next line. The class speaks the narrative, Piggy-wig says, 'I will'. The couple move away with the imaginary ring towards the Turkey. They mime the eating of an imaginary meal, and then Owl and Pussy-Cat perform some kind of slow dance.

THE POBBLE WHO HAS NO TOES: EDWARD LEAR (p. 14)

AIM. To appreciate the way in which the rhythm of the lines suits the sheer absurdity of the poem.

INTRODUCTION. Read the poem to the class briskly and clearly. The demands are, of course, for a light touch. The sheer absurdity is well brought out by a grave and serious air. The strong beats in each line should be clearly marked.

> The Pobble who has no toes
>   Had once as many as we;
> When they said, 'Some day you may lose them all;'
>   He replied, 'Fish fiddle de-dee!'
> And his Aunt Jobiska made him drink,
> Lavender water tinged with pink,
> For she said, 'The World in general knows
>   There's nothing so good for a Pobble's toes!'

CHORAL READING. The class should be divided into two groups. Each group speaks a verse. It is a good poem for single speakers to try to speak. Encourage light, clear reading with a touch of gravity.

THE JUMBLIES: EDWARD LEAR (p. 16)

AIM. To appreciate through choral reading the various changes in rhythm in the poem.

INTRODUCTION. Read the poem to the class. Indicate clearly by changes of voice the four parts of the poem: the narrative; the lines

6

spoken by 'every one'; the lines spoken by the Jumblies; and the lines spoken by the chorus:

> Fár and féw, fár and féw,
> Are the lánds where the Júmblies líve;
> Their heáds are gréen, and their hánds are blúe,
> And they wént to séa in a Síeve.

Bring out in your reading the smooth rhythm of the verse.

CHORAL READING. Divide the class into three groups. The first group will speak the narrative lines; the second group will speak for the Jumblies; the third group speaks for 'every one'. All three groups then join in the chorus beginning:

> 'Far and few, far and few.'

It is important that cues are taken up immediately, particularly where the narrative lines are followed by direct speech.

The whole poem should be read in a brisk and lively manner.

THE DONG WITH A LUMINOUS NOSE: EDWARD LEAR (p. 20)

AIM. To appreciate the lyrical qualities of this nonsense poem.

INTRODUCTION. Read the poem to the class after careful preparation. Try to bring out the delicate rhythm and the great variety of sound effects throughout the poem.

CHORAL READING. Divide the class as follows. The best reader should speak the words of the Dong throughout. A small group of about ten voices should speak the words of 'those who watch at that midnight hour' in the third and last stanzas. A large group should read the narrative. The whole class should join in the Jumblies Chorus in the fifth stanza.

The poem is full of lovely sounding words and phrases:

> 'When Storm-clouds brood on the towering heights
> Of the Hills of the Chankly Bore.'

. . .

7

'For the Jumblies came in a Sieve, they did,—
Landing at eve near the Zemmery Fidd.'

The poem must be spoken fairly slowly to give full value to the sound of the words.

THE AKOND OF SWAT: EDWARD LEAR (p. 23)

AIM. To appreciate the skilful rhythmic arrangement of this poem, and to enjoy the absurd way in which an eager thirst for knowledge is presented with impressive mock solemnity.

INTRODUCTION. Read the poem to the class showing how the variety of emphasis should be made. Read the poem a second time to show the importance to the general effect of pauses. Notice particularly the silent beat in the first line and before the last line in each verse:

Who, or why, or which, or what, (´)   Is the Ákond of SWAT?

Is he tall or short, or dark or fair?
Does he sit on a stool or a sofa or chair,   OR SQUAT,
                                 (´) The Ákond of Swat?

CHORAL READING. Divide the class into three groups. The first group speaks the first line, the second group the second (the first group the third line in the first verse). The third group takes the words in capitals, and all three groups join in the refrain.

Group I. Is he wise or foolish, young or old?
Group II. Does he drink his soup and his coffee cold,
Group III.   OR HOT
All together.   (´) The Ákond of Swat?

SECTION 2

PICTURES IN WORDS

THE EAGLE: LORD TENNYSON (p. 36)

AIM. To help the class to form clear mental images by a careful consideration of the words and sounds in the poem.

INTRODUCTION. Read the poem to the class slowly and impressively. Read the poem again, giving each word the fullest value to help the imagination to build up all that is suggested. The poem is a vivid statement about the eagle. The emphasis on each word should be as even as possible. Try to give the greatest weight in the first verse to the word 'stands'. Give emphasis to the words 'close' and 'ringed'. In the second verse we are beside the eagle on the crag. The 'wrinkled sea' crawls far beneath us. Then the eagle swoops. Let the class be conscious of the slower movement of the line:

'He watches from his mountain-walls.'

Emphasize the pause after the word 'thunderbolt' to bring out as strongly as possible the last two words 'he falls'. The whole poem has been leading up to this dramatic movement.

DISCUSSION. Though the poem is short it is powerful. In order to realize fully the vivid qualities of the imagery discuss with the class the use of certain words and phrases.

Why 'clasps' and 'crooked hands'? They help to personify the eagle, making it almost human with hands clasping the crag. We can then identify ourselves with the eagle more readily and enter into its existence. 'Lonely lands' suggest the isolation of the eagle removed to remote places, brooding over its solitary kingdom. 'Crag' suggests height, an idea supported by the whole of the second line and made still more vivid by the words 'ringed with the azure world'. The word 'stands' suggests the dignity and calm supremacy of the eagle in his world of blue sky.

9

Why 'wrinkled sea'? First, it is an arresting word, then it suggests height from which the eagle looks down. We are now with the eagle and watch from his mountain walls. The word 'walls' continues the idea of kingdom suggested in the first stanza.

Why 'thunderbolt'? It is a powerful word, and by its sound and associations suggests the suddenness of the eagle's fall.

ILLUSTRATION. Draw the eagle as suggested to your imagination by the poet.

THE EAGLE: ANDREW YOUNG (p. 36)

AIM. To compare and contrast this poem with *The Eagle* by Tennyson.

INTRODUCTION. Read the poem to the class, and ask for general comments on first impressions. Read the poem a second time.

DISCUSSION COMPARING THE TWO POEMS. The following points may be brought out. Both poems consider the eagle as a bird of prey. Tennyson romanticizes the bird, regarding him as a king living in his kingdom of 'lonely lands'. We have a vivid series of pictures, and having considered the eagle on the height, then joined him in imagination we *share* the suddenness of his fall. Young considers less the scene, he concentrates on the narrow golden head 'scanning the ground to kill'. The point of the poem is found in the last two lines. Is the comparison found there effective? What is the implication? Perhaps that things are not what they seem. That the king of birds suffers also. And we are reminded of the King of men who was crucified.

SILVER: WALTER DE LA MARE (p. 37)

AIM. To appreciate the way in which the sounds suit the sense and enhance the scene.

INTRODUCTION. Read the poem to the class. This first reading is all important as it 'fixes the magic of sound and imagery'. The movement of the verse is full of variety and calls for great care in stress and phrasing. Show close attention to the precise meaning of the words.

INTERPRETATION. The poem opens slowly and quietly:

> Slówly, sílently, nów the moón
> Wálks the níght in her sílver shoón.

Notice how the distribution of stress and the long vowel sound in 'now' and 'moon' throws the stress on the first word, 'Walks', in the second line and carries the thought smoothly. The movement is varied in the third and fourth lines; the third line broken by pauses and by meaning, the fourth line carrying the sense complete.

> Thís wáy, ‖ and thát, ‖ she peérs, ‖ and seés
> Sílver frúit upon sílver treés.

The poem is built upon the word 'silver', and the soft sound of this word is supported by modulated vowel sounds and quiet consonants.

> 'From their shadowy cote the white breasts peep
> Of doves in a silver-feathered sleep.'

This fixes the way in which the poem should be read, its quietness suggesting the magic effect of moonlight.

THE POOR MAN'S PIG: EDMUND BLUNDEN (p. 39)

AIM. To appreciate the clarity and exactness of the word pictures in this poem.

INTRODUCTION. Read the poem to the class and ask for general comments on first impressions. Read the poem a second time bringing out the variety of pace. The poem opens slowly with its vivid description of the plum-bloom and the apple-boughs, and the building thrush watching old Job stacking 'fresh-peeled osiers.' The pace quickens with the lively description of the pig rushing out:

> 'in bundling gallop for the cottage door.'

The last line of the poem is read more slowly—

> 'And sulky as a child when her play's done.'

DISCUSSION. Try to bring out in general discussion the keen and sympathetic insight of the poet, and his remarkable eye for detail. *What passages of description are particularly effective?*

Comment on such expressions as:

> 'fallen plum-bloom *stars* the green'
> 'apple-boughs as *knarred* as old toads' backs'
> 'The *fresh-peeled* osiers on the sunny fence.'
> 'The pent sow grunts to hear him stumping by.'

Why is the word 'stumping' to describe old Job better than 'walking'?
What sort of picture does the phrase 'in bundling gallop' bring to mind?
What other word suggests the clumsy movement of the pig?

> 'Then like the whirlwind *bumping* round once more.'

ILLUSTRATION. The class may like to draw a picture of some of the images in the poem.

MILK FOR THE CAT: HAROLD MONRO (p. 40)

AIM. To appreciate the vivid way in which the cat is portrayed and to consider how the form of the poem suits the content.

INTRODUCTION. Read the poem to the class and ask for general comments on first impressions.

Read the poem again dealing with any difficulties of vocabulary.
agate: flecked with different colours like the semi-precious stone.
independent casual: free, easy.
lust: desire.

DISCUSSION

What is the theme of the first three stanzas? The quiet way in which the cat waits for its milk.

Where is the cat's sudden desire for milk described? In the next two stanzas. The expression of this desire reaches its climax in the line:

> 'Transformed to a creeping lust for milk.'

The next three stanzas describe the fulfilment of the cat's desire when:

> 'A long dim ecstasy holds her life.'

The last stanza describes the cat's final, complete contentment.

What phrases describe the cat most vividly?

'The little black cat with bright green eyes'

gives us an immediate picture. But notice also the effectiveness of:

'all her lithe body becomes
One breathing, trembling purr.'

And:
'each drowsy paw
Is doubled under each bending knee.'

What contrasts are made in the poem?

CHORAL READING. The poem is suitable for choral reading, when the class should try to bring out the growing excitement the cat feels in her desire for milk, the fulfilment of that desire and final satisfaction. Divide the class into four groups:

Group I to speak the first three stanzas.

Group II to speak the next two stanzas.

Group III to speak the next three stanzas.

Group IV to speak the last stanza.

WINTER: WILLIAM SHAKESPEARE (p. 44)

AIM. To appreciate the vividness of the imagery in this description of winter.

INTRODUCTION. Read the poem bringing out the lyrical movement of the lines. Read the poem again and explain the meaning of certain words:

keel: skim.

saw: a wise saying.

crabs: crab-apples.

DISCUSSION

Why does Dick the shepherd 'blow his nail'?

What is meant by 'blood is nipped'?

Why are the ways described as 'foul'?

Why is the line:

'And birds sit brooding in the snow'

so effective? Because it not only gives a vivid picture but the long open vowel sounds in 'brooding' and 'snow' suggest the unhappiness of the birds.

13

What is the effect of the use of proper names—Dick, Tom, Joan, Marian? It makes the scene more human and familiar.

What contrasts are made in the poem? The bitter cold outside and in the unheated church, and the warmth where Joan 'keels the pot' and 'roasted crabs hiss in the bowl'.

CHORAL READING. The poem may be read very effectively as follows:

Divide the class into three groups.

Stanza I and *Stanza II*.

Group I speaks lines 1 and 2.

Group II speaks lines 3 and 4.

Group III speaks lines 5 and 6.

The whole class joins in the refrain.

MISS THOMPSON GOES SHOPPING: MARTIN ARMSTRONG (p. 45)

AIM. To appreciate the accuracy of the poet's observation and the originality of the poetic description.

INTRODUCTION. Read the poem to the class bringing out the force and neatness of the images. Point the lines to emphasize the imagery.

Read the poem a second time, and then deal with any difficulties of vocabulary which may arise.

DISCUSSION. Lead the discussion from the character of Miss Thompson to the vivid and amusing observation shown in the description of the fishmonger's shop.

Which are the most striking pieces of description?

What comparisons are particularly effective?

Give examples of any rhymes which are rather humorous in their effect.

ILLUSTRATION. This description of the fishmonger's shop is so exact and original that it should be a most attractive subject for illustration. Something which is everyday and rather uninspiring suddenly becomes exciting and dramatic. This should encourage children to look on ordinary objects with livelier interest.

The class may be encouraged to write ten or twelve lines in verse on a similar subject using this poem as a model.

SECTION 3

TALES AND MINSTRELSY

GREEN BROOM: TRADITIONAL (p. 50)

AIM. To appreciate the theme of the narrative and more especially the unusual way the story is told.

INTRODUCTION. Read the poem to the class bringing out the liveliness of the rhythm. Ask the class for suggestions how the poem should be read in chorus.

CHORAL READING. Divide the class. The best reader should take the narrative lines, other good readers to read the parts of John, his father and the lady. The rest of the class say in unison the repetitions at the end of the second and fourth lines and all the fifth lines.

DRAMATIC WORK. The parts of John, his father and the lady should be strongly differentiated. The three parts may be acted at the front of the class so giving a dramatic rendering. With a little practice the poem, given in this way, should be both lively and entertaining. Practise especially quickness on the cues; and the unison at the end of each stanza must really be a unison.

THE FOX JUMPED UP ON A MOONLIGHT NIGHT: TRADITIONAL (p. 52)

AIM. To appreciate the liveliness of the tale and to practise dramatic presentation.

INTRODUCTION. Read the poem to the class bringing out the character of the fox as a fine swaggering fellow, and that of old Gammer Hipple-Hopple (as her name implies) as a crotchety and complaining old woman.

DRAMATIC WORK. A single speaker should take the part of the fox following the pattern already set. Another speaker should take the

15

part of old Gammer Hipple-Hopple and should speak in a high-pitched voice.

Divide the rest of the class into two groups:

Group I speaks the narrative in the first two verses, including the words 'said the fox'.

Group II should speak the narrative in the next two verses, Group I joining in the last line:

'And the young ones picked the bones, O.'

THE FROLICSOME DUKE: TRADITIONAL (p. 54)

AIM. To compare briefly the story of the 'Frolicsome Duke' as told by an old English writer with the lively way it is told in the ballad.

INTRODUCTION. Read to the class this account of an incident in the life of Philip the Good.

The story is told of Philip the Good, Duke of Burgundy; and is thus related by an old English writer:

'The said duke, at the marriage of Eleonora, sister to the King of Portugall, at Bruges in Flanders, which was solemnised in the deepe of winter; when as by reason of unseasonable weather he could neither hawke nor hunt, and was now tired with cards, dice, etc. and such other domestick sports, or to see ladies dance; with some of his courtiers, he would in the evening walke disguised all about the towne. It so fortuned as he was walking late one night, he found a countrey fellow dead drunke, snorting on a bulke; he caused his followers to bring him to his palace, and there stripping him of his old clothes, and attyring him after the court fashion, when he wakened he and they were all ready to attend upon his excellency, and to persuade him that he was some great duke. The poor fellow admiring how he came there was served in state all day long: after supper he saw them dance, heard musicke, and all the rest of those court-like pleasures: but late at night, when he was well tipled, and again fast asleepe, they put on his old robes, and so conveyed him to the place where they first found him. Now the fellow had not made them so good sport the day before, as he did now, when he returned to himself: all the jest was to see how he looked upon it. In conclusion, after some little admiration, the poore man told his friends he had seen a vision; constantly believed it; would not otherwise be persuaded, and so the jest ended.'

Then read the ballad version of the story.

DISCUSSION. Ask the class what the main differences are, and lead the discussion to a brief consideration of the rhythm of the poem, and the use of rhyme and repetition.

THE PIED PIPER OF HAMELIN: ROBERT BROWNING (p. 70)

AIM. To appreciate the dramatic qualities of this legendary tale, the variety of mood and the vivid, picturesque language.

INTRODUCTION. Read the poem to the class with as lively a tone of voice as possible so as to bring the characters to life and to do justice to the vigour of the words and rhythm. The poem contains both excitement and strangeness, homeliness and mystery, and demands careful interpretation.

DRAMATIZATION OF THE POEM. Divide the class into two large groups, one group to read the Chorus, the other the People. Individual readers take the other parts as indicated.

It is very important that the Mayor, the Piper and the Lame Child should be strongly differentiated. The class should gain some idea of the characters in the poem from the first reading.

Discuss briefly how these various characters should be presented.

The Mayor is greedy: probably also lazy, stupid and yet cunning. The Piper is a strange mysterious figure, with a grave, courteous manner and a sense of power because of his secret knowledge. The Mayor is impatient, with loud, blustering ways. Bring out the indignation and determination of the group of People who threaten the Mayor and Corporation.

Though characters are not so fully portrayed in poetry reading as in a play, they must be clearly suggested and presented as vividly as possible.

I am indebted to Mr A. S. T. Fisher (*Voice and Verse*, Part I)
for the following arrangement of the poem for dramatic presentation:

Narrator. Hamelin Town's in Brunswick,
    By famous Hanover city;
The river Weser, deep and wide,
Washes its wall on the southern side;
A pleasanter spot you never spied;
    But, when begins my ditty,
Almost five hundred years ago,
To see the townsfolk suffer so
    From vermin, was a pity.

Chorus.   Rats!
They fought the dogs and killed the cats,
    And bit the babies in the cradles,
And ate the cheeses out of the vats,
    And licked the soup from the cooks' own ladles,
Split open the kegs of salted sprats,
Made nests inside men's Sunday hats
And even spoiled the women's chats
    By drowning their speaking
    With shrieking and squeaking
In fifty different sharps and flats.

Narrator. At last the people in a body
    To the Town Hall came flocking:
People.   ''Tis clear,'
Narrator.   cried they,
People.   'our Mayor's a noddy;
And as for our Corporation—shocking
To think we buy gowns lined with ermine
For dolts that can't or won't determine
What's best to rid us of our vermin!
You hope, because you're old and obese,
To find in the furry civic robe ease?
Rouse up, Sirs! Give your brains a racking
To find the remedy we're lacking,
Or, sure as fate, we'll send you packing!'

Narrator. At this the Mayor and Corporation
   Quaked with a mighty consternation.

   An hour they sate in council;
    At length the Mayor broke silence:
Mayor. 'For a guilder I'd my ermine gown sell,
    I wish I were a mile hence!
   It's easy to bid one rack one's brain—
   I'm sure my poor head aches again
   I've scratched it so, and all in vain.
   Oh for a trap, a trap, a trap!'
Narrator. Just as he said this, what should hap
   At the chamber door but a gentle tap?
Mayor. 'Bless us,'
Narrator.   cried the Mayor,
Mayor.   'what's that?'
Narrator. (With the Corporation as he sat,
   Looking little though wondrous fat;
   Nor brighter was his eye, nor moister
   Than a too-long-opened oyster,
   Save when at noon his paunch grew mutinous
   For a plate of turtle green and glutinous.)
Mayor. 'Only a scraping of shoes on the mat?
   Anything like the sound of a rat
   Makes my heart go pit-a-pat!'

   'Come in!'
Narrator.   —the Mayor cried, looking bigger:
   And in did come the strangest figure!
   His queer long coat from heel to head
   Was half of yellow and half of red;
   And he himself was tall and thin,
   With sharp blue eyes, each like a pin,
   And light loose hair, yet swarthy skin,
   No tuft on cheek nor beard on chin,
   But lips where smiles went out and in—
   There was no guessing his kith and kin!

And nobody could enough admire
The tall man and his quaint attire.
Quoth one:

Councillor.   'It's as my great-grandsire,
Starting up at the Trump of Doom's tone,
Had walked this way from his painted tomb-stone!'

Narrator. He advanced to the council-table:
And,
Piper.   'Please your honours,'
Narrator.   said he,
Piper.   'I'm able,
By means of a secret charm, to draw
   All creatures living beneath the sun,
   That creep or swim or fly or run,
After me so as you never saw!
And I chiefly use my charm
On creatures that do people harm,
The mole and toad and newt and viper;
And people call me the Pied Piper.'
Narrator. (And here they noticed round his neck
   A scarf of red and yellow stripe,
To match with his coat of the self-same cheque;
   And at the scarf's end hung a pipe;
And his fingers, they noticed, were ever straying
As if impatient to be playing
Upon this pipe, as low it dangled
Over his vesture so old-fangled.)
Piper.   'Yet,'
Narrator.   said he,
Piper.   'poor piper as I am,
In Tartary I freed the Cham,
   Last June, from his huge swarms of gnats;
I eased in Asia the Nizam
   Of a monstrous brood of vampyre bats:
And as for what your brain bewilders,
   If I can rid your town of rats
Will you give me a thousand guilders?'
Mayor and Corporation. 'One? fifty thousand!'

20

Narrator.   —was the exclamation
         Of the astonished Mayor and Corporation.

Chorus.   Into the street the piper stept,
               Smiling first a little smile,
             As if he knew what magic slept
               In his quiet pipe the while;
             Then, like a musical adept,
             To blow the pipe his lips he wrinkled,
             And green and blue his sharp eyes twinkled,
             Like a candle-flame where salt is sprinkled;
             And ere three shrill notes the pipe uttered,
             You heard as if an army muttered;
             And the muttering grew to a grumbling;
             And the grumbling grew to a mighty rumbling;
             And out of the houses the rats came tumbling.
             Great rats, small rats, lean rats, brawny rats,
             Brown rats, black rats, grey rats, tawny rats,
             Grave old plodders, gay young friskers,
               Fathers, mothers, uncles, cousins,
             Cocking tails and pricking whiskers,
               Families by tens and dozens,
             Brothers, sisters, husbands, wives—
             Followed the Piper for their lives.
             From street to street he piped advancing,
             And step for step they followed dancing,
             Until they came to the river Weser
               Wherein all plunged and perished!
             —Save one who, stout as Julius Caesar,
             Swam across and lived to carry
               (As he, the manuscript he cherished)
             To Rat-land home his commentary:
             Which was,
Rat.   'At the first shrill notes of the pipe,
             I heard a sound as of scraping tripe,
             And putting apples, wondrous ripe,
             Into a cider-press's gripe:
             And a moving away of pickle-tub-boards,
             And a leaving ajar of conserve-cupboards,

And a drawing the corks of train-oil-flasks,
And a breaking the hoops of butter-casks;
And it seemed as if a voice
  (Sweeter far than by harp or by psaltery
Is breathed) called out, Oh rats, rejoice!
  The World is grown to one vast drysaltery!
So munch on, crunch on, take your nuncheon,
Breakfast, supper, dinner, luncheon!
And just as a bulky sugar-puncheon,
All ready staved, like a great sun shone
Glorious scarce an inch before me,
Just as methought it said, Come, bore me!
—I found the Weser rolling o'er me.'

Narrator. You should have heard the Hamelin people
  Ring the bells till they rocked the steeple.
Mayor. 'Go,'
Narrator.   cried the Mayor,
Mayor.   'and get long poles!
Poke out the nests and block up the holes!
  Consult with carpenters and builders,
And leave in our town not even a trace
Of the rats!'
Narrator.   —when suddenly, up the face
Of the Piper perked in the market-place,
  With a,
Piper.   'First, if you please, my thousand guilders!'

Narrator. A thousand guilders! The Mayor looked blue;
  So did the Corporation too.
For council dinners made rare havoc
With Claret, Moselle, Vin-de-Grave, Hock;
And half the money would replenish
Their cellar's biggest butt with Rhenish.
To pay this sum to a wandering fellow
With a gipsy coat of red and yellow!
Mayor. 'Beside,'
Narrator.   quoth the Mayor, with a knowing wink,
Mayor. 'Our business was done at the river's brink;

We saw with our eyes the vermin sink,
And what's dead can't come to life, I think.
So, friend, we're not the folks to shrink
From the duty of giving you something for drink,
And a matter of money to put in your poke;
But as for the guilders, what we spoke
Of them, as you very well know, was in joke.
Besides, our losses have made us thrifty,
A thousand guilders! Come, take fifty!'

Narrator. The piper's face fell, and he cried,
Piper.   'No trifling! I can't wait, beside!
I've promised to visit by dinner time
Bagdad, and accept the prime
Of the Head-Cook's pottage, all he's rich in,
For having left, in the Caliph's kitchen,
Of a nest of scorpions no survivor—
With him I proved no bargain-driver,
With you, don't think I'll bate a stiver!
And folks who put me in a passion
May find me pipe to another fashion.'

Mayor.   'How?'
Narrator.   cried the Mayor,
Mayor.   'd'ye think I'll brook
Being worse treated than a Cook?
Insulted by a lazy ribald
With idle pipe and vesture piebald?
You threaten us, fellow? Do your worst,
Blow your pipe there till you burst!

Chorus. Once more he stept into the street;
        And to his lips again
        Laid his long pipe of smooth straight cane;
And ere he blew three notes (such sweet
Soft notes as yet musician's cunning
Never gave the enraptured air)
There was a rustling that seemed like a bustling
Of merry crowds justling at pitching and hustling,

23

Small feet were pattering, wooden shoes clattering,
Little hands clapping and little tongues chattering,
And, like fowls in a farm-yard when barley is scattering,
Out came the children running.
All the little boys and girls,
With rosy cheeks and flaxen curls,
And sparkling eyes and teeth like pearls,
Tripping and skipping, ran merrily after
The wonderful music with shouting and laughter.

Narrator. The Mayor was dumb, and the Council stood
As if they were changed into blocks of wood,
Unable to move a step, or cry
To the children merrily skipping by—
Could only follow with the eye
That joyous crowd at the Piper's back.
But how the Mayor was on the rack
And the wretched Council's bosoms beat,
As the Piper turned from the High Street
To where the Weser rolled its waters
Right in the way of their sons and daughters!
However he turned from South to West,
And to Koppelberg Hill his steps addressed,
And after him the children pressed;
Great was the joy in every breast.
People. 'He never can cross that mighty top!
He's forced to let the piping drop,
And we shall see our children stop!'
Narrator. When, lo, as they reached the mountain's side,
A wondrous portal opened wide,
As if a cavern was suddenly hollowed;
And the Piper advanced and the children followed,
And when all were in to the very last,
The door in the mountain-side shut fast.
Did I say all? No! One was lame,
    And could not dance the whole of the way;
And in after years, if you would blame
    His sadness, he was used to say,—

24

Lame   'It's dull in our town since my playmates left!
Child.   I can't forget that I'm bereft
     Of all the pleasant sights they see,
     Which the Piper also promised me.
     For he led us, he said, to a joyous land,
     Joining the town and just at hand,
     Where waters gushed and fruit-trees grew,
     And flowers put forth a fairer hue,
     And everything was strange and new;
     The sparrows were brighter than peacocks here,
     And their dogs outran our fallow deer,
     And honey-bees had lost their stings,
     And horses were born with eagles' wings:
     And just as I became assured
     My lame foot would be speedily cured,
     The music stopped and I stood still,
     And found myself outside the Hill,
     Left alone against my will,
     To go now limping as before,
     And never hear of that country more!...'

Narrator. Alas, alas for Hamelin!
       There came into many a burgher's pate
       A text which says, that Heaven's Gate
       Opes to the Rich at as easy rate
     As the needle's eye takes the camel in!
     The Mayor sent East, West, North and South,
     To offer the Piper, by word of mouth,
       Wherever it was men's lot to find him,
     Silver and gold to his heart's content,
     If he'd only return the way he went,
       And bring the children behind him.
     But when they saw 'twas a lost endeavour,
     And Piper and dancers were gone for ever,
     They made a decree that lawyers never
       Should think their records dated duly
     If, after the day of the month and year,
     These words did not as well appear,
     'And so long after what happened here

On the Twenty-second of July,
Thirteen hundred and seventy-six':
And better in memory to fix
The place of the children's last retreat,
They called it the Pied Piper's Street—
Where any one playing on pipe or tabor
Was sure for the future to lose his labour.
Nor suffered they hostelry or tavern
　　To shock with mirth a street so solemn;
But opposite the place of the cavern
　　They wrote the story on a column,
And on the great Church Window painted
The same, to make the world acquainted
How their children were stolen away;
And there it stands to this very day.
And I must not omit to say
That in Transylvania there's a tribe
Of alien people that ascribe
The outlandish ways and dress
On which their neighbours lay such stress,
To their fathers and mothers having risen
Out of some subterraneous prison
Into which they were trepanned
Long time ago in a mighty band
Out of Hamelin town in Brunswick land,
But how or why, they don't understand.

So, Willy, let you and me be wipers
Of scores out with all men—especially pipers:
And, whether they pipe us free, from rats or from mice,
If we've promised them aught, let us keep our promise.

THE JACKDAW OF RHEIMS: R. H. BARHAM (p. 79)

AIM. To appreciate the animated conversational style of this poem.

INTRODUCTION. Read the poem, bringing out the neat polished
effect of the phrases, and the contrast between the impudence of the
Jackdaw and the dignity of the Cardinal. Try to show the variety of
rhythm—the excited agitation of the people searching for the ring

rising from one climax to another—the solemn slowness of the passage beginning:

> . 'The Cardinal rose with a dignified look.'

Intonation should be animated, the opening lines should not be spoken loudly but should move briskly.

After the first reading deal with some difficulties of vocabulary:

cope and pall: outer vestments.
rochet: abbot's surplice.

DRAMATIC PRESENTATION. Divide the class: a single voice to take the words of the Jackdaw, another those of the Abbot.

One group should form a chorus of priests, monks and friars.

Another group of six should represent the six singing-boys. Each member of the group speaks the lines which concern him.

Certain sections must be spoken quickly and loudly. The fourth section should be spoken in this way up to the words 'THE RING', which should be spoken very loudly.

Variation should be made by beginning the lines:

> 'He cursed him at board, he cursed him in bed...'

very quietly and slowly. Then speak faster and louder to the line:

> 'Never was heard such a terrible curse!!'

This should be followed by a sudden pause to bring out the anti-climax of the next three lines:

> 'But what gave rise
> To no little surprise,
> Nobody seem'd one penny the worse!'

THE POET'S FEELING

THE FIDDLER OF DOONEY: W. B. YEATS (p. 86)

AIM. To consider carefully the thought behind the poem, that a merry heart is more blessed than a mind given to prayer.

INTRODUCTION. Read the poem to the class bringing out the lyrical movement of the lines.

Read the poem again explaining how important the fair is in Irish country life, and how the fiddler is a familiar and respected figure at the fair.

DISCUSSION. Though the language of the poem is very simple the thought behind it is quite profound.

What is the theme of the poem? The theme is put plainly in the fourth verse:

'For the good are always the merry,
Save by an evil chance',

and this thought is extended—

'And the merry love the fiddle
And the merry love to dance.'

What is implied in the first verse about the fiddler's playing? It was *merry* playing for it made

'Folk dance like a wave of the sea.'

Having established this fact the poet says that his cousin 'is priest in Kilvarnet' and his brother, also a priest, lives in Moharabuiee.

How are the cousin and brother joined together in the second verse? They both read in their books of prayer.

How is the fiddler made to differ from them? He reads in his book of songs.

What is meant by:

'When we come at the end of time'?

When we come to Judgment Day.

28

Why does Peter 'sitting in state' call the fiddler first *through the gate, before his brother or his cousin, the priests?* Because he was so merry on earth and the 'good are always merry'. Therefore he is the best of the three and deserves to go first through the gate.

What is the effect of the fiddler on the people in heaven when they see him? They welcome him as they had done on earth, and when he plays again they

'dance like a wave of the sea.'

TO THE CUCKOO: WILLIAM WORDSWORTH (p. 87)

AIM. To appreciate the expression of the poet's feeling and to consider the experience behind it.

INTRODUCTION. Read the poem paying particular attention to the feeling of joy in the poem. Read the poem again. Explain briefly how the memories of childhood are enriched by the passing of time, and how easily they may be revived by a chance sight or sound.

DISCUSSION
What is the poem about?
Which parts of the poem describe the cuckoo?
How much is said about the cuckoo? Only the voice, 'the two-fold shout', is mentioned.
How does the poet express his sense of wonder?
What words show the joyousness of the experience?

'O blithe newcomer!'...'darling of the Spring.'

What are the associations brought before the poet by the cuckoo's song? Lying on grass; babbling only to the vale; of sunshine and of flowers—all suggesting freedom from care.

The association of the cuckoo is with childhood. It is a recollected experience from the distant past. The poet is listening to the sound of the cuckoo, but this is not the first thing he mentions, 'I have heard...'. He returns to the thought expressed here later in the poem.

Where? How did the bird appear to him then? Did he see it?

> 'And thou wert still a hope, a love,
>   Still long'd for, never seen!'

How do the past years when he heard the cuckoo live in his imagination?
> 'Visionary hours; that golden time.'

He remembers the time when he was a child, but he does far more than that. He recalls the same kind of *joy* that he had in his childhood.

THE DARKLING THRUSH: THOMAS HARDY (p. 88)

AIM. To try to understand the feeling of the poet expressed in the poem and by comparison with *To the Cuckoo* to increase appreciation of each poem.

INTRODUCTION. Read the poem to the class. Read the poem a second time.

DISCUSSION. Hardy does not describe the thrush but the landscape which expresses his own mood.

What words suggest gloom? 'Spectre-gray', 'Winter's dregs'; 'weakening eye of day'; 'scored the sky'; 'broken lyres'.

What suggests the date of the poem? 'Century's corpse': end of the nineteenth century.

Why 'sharp features'? Bareness of winter; associations of death.

What other suggestions of death are there? 'Shrunken hard and dry.'

COMPARISON WITH 'TO THE CUCKOO'. Hardy describes the appearance of the thrush. Wordsworth mentions only the song of the cuckoo.

Suggest reasons for the description of the bird in *The Darkling Thrush*.

The dilapidated appearance of the thrush emphasizes the contrast with its song and with its surroundings.

What was the effect of the song of the cuckoo on Wordsworth?
What was the effect of the song of the thrush on Hardy?

Read the last stanza of *To the Cuckoo* and the last stanza of *The Darkling Thrush*. Read both poems again.

AN OLD WOMAN OF THE ROADS: PADRAIC COLUM (p. 90)

AIM. To extend the imaginative experience of the class by appreciating sympathetically the feelings of the old woman in the poem.

INTRODUCTION. Read the poem to the class bringing out the sense of loneliness of the old woman and her longing for the comfort and security of a house of her own.

Read the poem a second time.

DISCUSSION. The questions should follow the development of the theme. The first two stanzas describe the house she longs for and the things she wishes to own.

How does it differ from the houses we know? 'Heaped-up sods', 'pile of turf'.

What do we gather from this?

Would it be a pleasant house to live in?

The next two stanzas describe what would keep the old woman busy in the house.

What activities show her pride in this house?

The last two stanzas describe her present life.

Why is she so unhappy?

What lines describe her loneliness?

What strong contrast do we find in this poem? A contrast between the old woman's life as it is and as she would like it to be.

Read the poem once again.

THE LAMB: WILLIAM BLAKE (p. 92)

AIM. To consider two poems which have a similar theme but are different in presentation and in detail; to discover the similarity so that each poem may illuminate the other.

INTRODUCTION. Read the poem to the class and ask for general comments on first impressions.

DISCUSSION. It is useful to get suggestions from the class on the way in which this poem should be read. Such suggestions often show quite good judgment and understanding of the poem. There may be several ways of reading the poem and these may be tried to find the most effective one. It will be agreed that the poem must be read by a single voice quietly and with a sense of humility and of wonder. The class must consider the best way of expressing the question and answer kind of poem, and how to give the proper emphasis to the repetitions which open and close both stanzas in this poem. Bring out, above all, the sense of innocent wonder in this poem which will serve as a strong contrast to the sense of terror in *The Tyger*.

THE TYGER: WILLIAM BLAKE (p. 92)

AIM. To appreciate the vivid phrasing of the poem, the use of the question and the intensity of the poet's feeling. Also to feel the fierce terror of the poem and compare it with *The Lamb*.

INTRODUCTION. Read the poem to the class with some intensity and emphasize strongly the consonants. This emphasis is set in the first line:

Tyger! Tyger! burning bright.

Read the poem a second time and ask the class for general comments on first impressions.

DISCUSSION. Use the method of questions and commentary on each stanza. Also ask for suggestions on the way in which the poem should be read.

STANZA I

Which words in the first line demand special emphasis? 'Burning bright', because they make the tiger a living, wild and dangerous animal. The two words are also joined by the explosive consonant, 'b'.

How does the poet imagine the tiger? As a wild animal living in the jungle. Here he is isolated in the imagination 'the forests of the night'.

Which words in the last two lines suggest how the lines should be read? 'Fearful', 'immortal hand could frame'—all giving the idea of fear. Try to show this in the reading. Notice the spelling of the word 'tiger'. Does 'Tyger' suggest that this is no ordinary tiger such as one might see in the Zoo; but a beast combining all the terror of all tigers? There should be a slight pause in reading after the words 'hand' and 'eye' in line 3 to emphasize them. They are important words because they lead to the description of the fashioning of the tiger in the next stanzas. 'Eye' is, of course, that of the Creator. Explain how we speak of seeing things in the mind's eye, how often we see things in that way before drawing a picture or making a model. The next three stanzas tell us about the fashioning of the tiger.

STANZA II

What is the key-word of the first two lines? Fire. This is the substance from which the eyes of the tiger are made.

What two words in the first line are linked together by sound? 'Distant deeps'. Note how this linking of sound is a feature of the poem.

What quality of the Creator is emphasized? Courage and daring.

STANZA III

In this stanza the tiger's body is described.

What word in the first line is most important? Shoulder. This is the word indicating the strength of the body. Note the vigour in the words 'twist' and 'sinews', and how the words 'began to beat' in the third line suggest the throbbing of the tiger's heart.

STANZA IV

What is the theme of this stanza? Making the tiger's brain.

Where is it made? In the forge. Note the violence and fear associated with the word 'furnace'.

What particular quality is needed to make the brain of the tiger? Superhuman strength. A strength which could overcome fear. Note the three heavily stressed words at the end of the third line: 'what dread grasp'; and the phrase 'deadly terrors' in line 4.

STANZA V

The fashioning of the tiger is complete. The whole universe is conscious of the new creation. The stars weep with sorrow at what has been done. God makes both the fierce, terrible creatures like the tiger and gentle creatures like the lamb. The poet can hardly believe that this is possible.

STANZA VI

The first and the last stanzas are similar but there is *one* difference. *What is it?* 'Could' has been changed now to 'dare'. The poet can hardly believe that the Creator of the lamb could *dare* to create the tiger. He is deeply troubled by this contradiction.

Read through the poem again to bring out the full force of all the points raised in the discussion, and to show how different it is from the calm serenity of *The Lamb*.

THE BELLS OF HEAVEN: RALPH HODGSON (p. 95)

AIM. To sense and share the poet's feeling of pity for the suffering of animals.

INTRODUCTION. Read the poem to the class and ask for general comments on first impressions. Read the poem again emphasizing the word 'angry' in the sixth line.

DISCUSSION

What is the theme of the poem? The poet's anger at man's ill-treatment of animals.

What, says the poet, would ring the bells of Heaven? If the Parson and the people knelt down with angry prayers for ill-treated animals.

What strikes you as unusual about these prayers? They are *angry* prayers, and they are for tigers, dogs, bears, pit-ponies and hares.

What do you notice about the animals the poet mentions? They are all unhappy. The tigers are in captivity 'tamed and shabby', the dogs and bears are performing unnaturally, the pit-ponies are wretched and blind, and the hares are hunted. Notice the misery suggested in the words the poet uses—'shabby', 'wretched', 'blind' and 'hunted'.

Do you think the appeal for us to come to our senses is justified?

Read the poem again to give force to the points raised in the discussion.

PART II

THE POET'S SONG

COME UNTO THESE YELLOW SANDS:
WILLIAM SHAKESPEARE (p. 101)

AIM. To catch something of the magic of words beyond their plain prose meaning in reading this lyrical poem.

INTRODUCTION. Place the song in its proper setting in *The Tempest*. Explain that Ferdinand, the son of the King of Naples, having saved himself from the shipwreck, is weeping because he believes that his father has been drowned. Suddenly he hears the music of Ariel, a spirit of the island:

> 'This music crept by me upon the waters,
> Allaying both their fury and my passion
> With its sweet air.'

He has risen and is following the sound.

> 'Come unto these yellow sands...'

is the song the invisible Ariel sings, and Ferdinand, hardly understanding the words, tries to find the singer.

The song appears to be an invitation to dance. Read the poem to the class.

CHORAL READING. Shakespeare directed that the burden (or undersong) should be said 'dispersedly within', that is from different parts of the stage. The words Bow, wow (forming the burden) should be spoken by three single voices and should come from different parts of the class following one after the other. To gain the effect of fading in the distance each one should be fainter in sound than the one before.

Various members of the class should read the poem paying particular attention to the vowel sounds, these give much of the music to the verse and should be clearly spoken.

When the class is familiar with the sound of the words, and can give full value to the vowels, divide into groups for choral reading as follows:

Group I, lines 1 and 2.
Group II, lines 3 and 4.
Group III, lines 5 and 6.

Single Voice.   Hark! Hark!
Burden.   Bow, wow (*three single voices from different parts of the room*).

Single Voice.   The watch-dogs bark.
Burden.   Bow, wow (*as before*).
Single Voice.   Hark! Hark! I hear
                 The strain of strutting chanticleer
                 Cry
Second shriller
single voice.   Cock-a-diddle-dow!

THE ECHOING GREEN: WILLIAM BLAKE (p. 104)

AIM. To appreciate the sound of the words and to see how well they fit the picture of a perfect spring day.

INTRODUCTION. Read the poem, ask for general comments on first impressions. Read the poem again.

DISCUSSION

What natural progression do you find in this poem? It describes a spring day from sunrise to dark.

What signs of joy are in the poem? The skies are happy; the bells and the birds seem to compete with each other; Old John laughs away care; the old folk laugh watching the children at play and re-live their own childhood.

In what way is the poem a complete and satisfying whole? Because of the natural progression of the day—'the Sun does arise' is balanced by 'the sun does descend', the 'birds of the bush' in the opening verse are recalled in the last verse in the comparison 'Like birds in their nest', the 'Echoing Green' of the beginning

38

becomes the 'darkening Green' in the last line. The poem will repay careful examination in this way.

Discuss the way in which the poem should be read. You will notice that in the first verse there are two stresses in each line:

> The Sun does arise,
> And make happy the skies;
> The merry bells ring
> To welcome the Spring;
> The skylark and thrush,
> The birds of the bush,
> Sing louder around
> To the bells' cheerful sound,
> While our sports shall be seen
> On the Echoing Green.

In the second verse the speech of the old folk has three stresses in each line to give the effect of the slow speech of old people:

> 'Such, such were the joys
> When we all, girls and boys,
> In our youth-time were seen
> On the Echoing Green.'

The verse is given variety by the way all the lines end with a strong stress in the first two stanzas, and in the third stanza lines 1, 2, 5 and 6 end with a weak or unaccented syllable:

> Till the little ones, weary,
> No more can be merry;
> The sun does descend,
> And our sports have an end.
> Round the laps of their mothers
> Many sisters and brothers,

39

Like birds in their nest,
Are ready for rest,
And sport no more seen
On the darkening Green.

After discussion divide the class into three groups for choral reading:

Stanza I: Group I (*light voices*).
Stanza II: Group II (*light voices*).
Stanza III: Group III (*heavy voices*).

BLOW, BLOW, THOU WINTER WIND:
WILLIAM SHAKESPEARE (p. 108)

AIM. To gain some appreciation of the sound of the words in the poem and to arouse some feeling for the theme, 'man's ingratitude'.

INTRODUCTION. Explain briefly the situation in *As You Like It* when Amiens sings this song. The banished Duke and his lords are living like outlaws in the Forest of Arden. Orlando, escaping from his brother, is in distress and rushes into the presence of the Duke with drawn sword. He is received kindly, and invited to eat with the others. Then Amiens sings this song, which bears on the misfortunes of the Duke and of Orlando.

Read the poem with vigour.

CHORAL READING. Divide the class into two groups, one to read the first verse, the other the second verse and both groups joining in the refrain.

The poem needs to be considered carefully before any attempt at choral reading is made. The interpretation should have boldness and energy. Though the exile lords are living in a forest under hardships of weather and physical discomforts they are not in despair and instead are defiant and ready to outface the elements.

The whole reading, therefore, should be strong and sustained, the keynote being taken from the first line:

'Blow, blow, thou winter wind.'

A difficulty will be to give vigour to the enunciation of the short vowel sounds in winter. This contrast between the long vowel sounds and more acute sounds is a feature of the poem:

> 'Thy tooth is not so keen,
> Because thou art not seen.'

Clarity of enunciation is demanded to keep the vigour of the reading, especially in the second verse:

> 'Freeze, freeze thou bitter sky.'

Notice the more even distribution of vowel sounds in the sixth line of each verse.

> 'Although thy breath be rude.'

and:

> 'As friend remember'd not.'

These lines should be spoken in a way to distinguish them from previous lines, perhaps on a deeper note and rather more slowly. The refrain should be spoken in a lively cheerful way, with a quick pace and a ringing tone.

NOW THE HUNGRY LION ROARS:
WILLIAM SHAKESPEARE (p. 109)

AIM. To gain an appreciation of the eeriness of the atmosphere through an imaginative understanding of the sense of the words and the sounds and rhythm of the verse.

INTRODUCTION. Explain briefly that these lines are spoken by Puck, or Robin Goodfellow, an impish spirit, in *A Midsummer Night's Dream*. It is night-time, the play is almost over, the mortals have left the stage and the immortals recapture the atmosphere of a dream (or a nightmare). Read the poem, first explaining that Hecate was the goddess of magic and of the moon. She appeared in three different shapes hence '*triple* Hecate's team'.

CHORAL READING. Divide the class into two groups, one with lighter and the other with heavier voices.

Group I (*heavier voices*) speaks the first twelve lines, down to '...paths to glide'.

Group II (*lighter voices*) speaks the next six lines, down to '...this hallowed house'.

The last two lines of the first section:

> 'I am sent with broom before,
> To sweep the dust behind the door'

should be spoken by a single voice.

The atmosphere of eeriness and nightmare should be kept in the opening lines by the first group. The reading of the second group should be less vigorous or intense. Changes of emphasis should be made throughout, and the single voice coming in at the end of the first section should read:

> 'not a mouse
> Shall disturb this hallow'd house'

with Group II so that he does not obtrude when he reads the last two lines alone.

Group II (*lighter voices*) speaks the first sixteen lines of the second section down to

> 'Ever shall be fortunate'

bringing out the delicate sound and graceful movement of the verse.

Group I (*heavier voices*) speaks the next fourteen lines down to

> 'Ever shall in safety rest'

giving full weight to the 'blots of Nature's hand'.

A single voice should speak the last three lines of the poem.

OVERHEARD ON A SALTMARSH: HAROLD MONRO (p. 110)

AIM. To try to gain an appreciation of the meaning and power of this fantasy and to understand the strongly contrasted characters in the poem.

INTRODUCTION. Read the poem to the class. Ask for suggestions how it should be read. It is a duet, and the poem may be interpreted in various ways.

The goblin at first asks for the beads because they look so attractive and he has taken a fancy to them. When he is asked why he wants them we find that he is both sensitive to beauty and highly imaginative. The nymph is not moved by his demand and refuses to give him the beads throughout the poem. Here is the contrast. The goblin who asks for the beads is drawn by their strange beauty, he speaks roughly, then passionately, finally violently. The nymph answers 'No' to each demand but in a changing tone. First calmly, then coldly; she says

'Hush, I stole them out of the moon'

in a teasing tone, and finally she is frightened for she cannot understand the goblin's persistence or feeling for her 'glass beads'.

CHORAL READING. This may be done with two single speakers, or with two small groups. The rhythm is not immediately obvious:

> Nýmph, nýmph, whát are your beáds?
> Gréen glass, góblin. Whý do you stáre at them?
> Gíve them me.
>   Nó.
> Gíve them me. Gíve them me.
>   Nó.

Usually four strong beats in the line, with occasionally two as above.

FULL FATHOM FIVE: WILLIAM SHAKESPEARE (p. 111)

AIM. To appreciate the sound effects of the words, what has been called the 'swell and lapse' of the tide in the first three lines, and the sound of the breaking waves in the fifth and sixth lines, and the lyrical quality of the whole poem.

INTRODUCTION. Explain briefly the situation in *The Tempest* where the song occurs. Prospero has caused a shipwreck near his island and it is part of his plan to let Ferdinand remain ignorant that his father has been saved from drowning. Here Ariel, who sings the song, is taunting Ferdinand who remarks:

> 'The ditty does remember my drown'd father:
> This is no mortal business, nor no sound
> That the earth owes.'

43

CHORAL READING. Read the poem to the class. The poem is very suitable for choral reading because it contains many long vowel sounds:

> 'Full fathom five thy father lies;
> Of his bones are coral made;
> Those are pearls that were his eyes.'

The 's' sound so skilfully used combined with the other sounds in these lines suggests the 'swell and lapse' of the tide.

In the lines:

> 'But doth suffer a sea-change
> Into something rich and strange'

the 's' sounds and the 'ch' and 'ge' and soft 'g' consonants suggest the 'pluck and knock' of the waves washing over the shingle.

Divide the class as follows:

Group I, line 1.
Group II (*lighter voices*), line 2.
Group I, line 3.
Group II (*light voices*), line 4.
Group I (*just above a whisper*), lines 5, 6 and 7.

Two or three voices.	Ding-dong.
Single voice.	Hark! now I hear them—
All together.	Ding-dong, bell.

THE NATURAL SCENE

SPRING: THOMAS NASHE (p. 117)

AIM. To appreciate the vivid word pictures of spring and to feel the liveliness of this descriptive poem.

INTRODUCTION. Read the poem to the class, and ask for general comments on first impressions. If the poem is read on a bright spring day the class might give some first-hand observations on the signs of spring. The poem consists of a series of clear simple pictures:

> 'then blooms each thing',
> 'then maids dance in a ring',
> 'lambs frisk and play',
> 'the shepherds pipe all day',
> 'old wives a-sunning sit'.

This should be visualized as clearly as possible.

What have the pictures in common? They are all fresh and gay, capturing the spirit of spring.

Read the poem again.

DISCUSSION

What birds are referred to in the poem by their calls? Cuckoo; *jug-jug*: nightingale; *pu-we*: plover or peewit; *to-witta-woo*: owl.

Which of the pictures in the poem should we not see today?

> 'Maids dance in a ring',
> 'The palm and may make country houses gay',
> 'The shepherds pipe all day.'

Which picture is the most vividly presented?

Mr A. S. T. Fisher, in his *Voice and Verse*, makes the following suggestion for 'Choral reading'. Divide the class into four groups and read the poem as follows:

Cuckoos.   The first line of each stanza.
Nightingales. The first half of the second line.

45

Peewits.　　The second half of the second line.

Owls.　　The third line.

In the fourth line each group makes the appropriate bird call. All four groups join in the final line of the poem:

'Spring, the sweet Spring!'

HOME-THOUGHTS, FROM ABROAD: ROBERT BROWNING (p. 117)

AIM. To visualize the pictures in this descriptive poem, and to feel the sharpened desire of the poet for home.

INTRODUCTION. Read the poem to the class. Read the poem a second time and explain that the poet was abroad in Italy and as his thoughts turned to home he recalls his delight in the English April. Imagine yourself in his place. If you felt an intense longing for the English spring wouldn't you try to remember the tiniest detail?

DISCUSSION

What are the details the poet describes? Tiny leaves round the elm-tree bole, pear-blossom falling from the tree that leans over the hedge into the field.

What bird song does he hear?

'The chaffinch sings on the orchard bough.'

This song is heard throughout April and May all over England.

'That's the wise thrush; he sings each song twice over.'

This is an exact description of the song of the thrush. Things are not only sharply and clearly seen but clearly *heard*. Notice how the poet shows us exactly where the thrush sits—'at the bent-spray's edge'.

In all his joy there is an undertone of sadness. He recalls the scene so vividly that for a moment he believes he is in England. Suddenly he sees a melon-flower that reminds him where he really is, and he shows his dislike of the flower by calling it 'gaudy'—not 'gay' like the English buttercups.

Which picture appeals to you most in this poem?

The poet has shown you an imaginative world. Illustrate the scene as you see it.

THE DAFFODILS: WILLIAM WORDSWORTH (p. 119)

AIM. To gather all the suggestions made by the poet and re-create the scene, then to share the experience expressed in the poem.

INTRODUCTION. Read the poem to the class. Then read the following passage from Dorothy Wordsworth's *Journal*. Wordsworth and his sister were returning from Eusemere to Dove Cottage in Grasmere.

'When we were in the woods beyond Gowbarrow Park we saw a few daffodils close to the water-side. We fancied that the lake had floated the seeds ashore, and that the little colony had so sprung up. But as we went along there were more and yet more; and at last, under the boughs of the trees, we saw that there was a long belt of them along the shore, about the breadth of a country turnpike road. I never saw daffodils so beautiful. They grew among the mossy stones about and about them; some rested their heads upon these stones as on a pillow for weariness; and the rest tossed and reeled and danced, and seemed as if they verily laughed with the wind, that blew upon them over the lake: they looked so gay, ever glancing, ever changing. This wind blew directly over the lake to them. There was here and there a little knot, and a few stragglers a few yards higher up, but they were so few as not to disturb the simplicity, unity and life of that one busy highway.'

Read the poem again.

DISCUSSION

What kind of landscape does the poet suggest? One which is bare and austere.

With what does he compare his own loneliness? With that of a cloud floating over vales and hills: this image fills in the scene; we are told merely of the lake and the trees.

What stands out brightly amid the spring scene? The daffodils: they provide the gay company.

How does the poet improve on the word 'crowd' in the first stanza? He calls the daffodils a 'host'—suggesting an army telling of the invasion of spring.

47

How many adjectives are used in the first stanza? One—golden. Note how this economy in the use of epithets makes the word 'golden' stand out—giving that warmth of colour which makes the scene leap to the eye.

What change of rhythm do you find in the first stanza? The last line has a dancing rhythm:

Fluttering and dancing in the breeze.

Why does the poet liken the daffodils to the stars in the Milky Way? Because of their number; it gives radiance also, and connects the great sweep of the stars with the arresting line of flowers and combines the crystal freshness with twinkling movement. The eye follows the 'tossing heads' along that far margin. If the poem were without this stanza we should lose the spaciousness of the scene.

Why does the poet call the daffodils a 'jocund' company? Jocund means merry. The word suggests that the flowers expressed their joy completely in the sparkling movement of the dance. Originally Wordsworth had used the word 'laughing'. By the change to 'jocund', sound, even of laughter, does not intrude upon the scene. The effect Wordsworth achieves is that of sparkling, joyful motion.

Why is 'gazed' a better word in line 5 of the third stanza than 'watched'? Suggests being lost in thought.

What word in the first stanza does 'wealth' recall? Golden: this, however, is a different kind of wealth.

What does 'vacant' mean? Thinking of nothing in particular.

What is the meaning of 'inward eye'? The mind's eye; the visual imagination. Here one can recall what one has seen. This, says the poet, is the 'bliss of solitude'.

What words suggest the suddenness with which the scene may be recalled? 'Flash'—suggests not only the suddenness but also the ease with which one can re-live a happy experience, for the poet says:

'And then my heart with pleasure fills,
And dances with the daffodils.'

What feeling is the final expression of the poet in this poem? That of happiness. An emotion comparable to the one he felt when he first saw the daffodils.

48

PIED BEAUTY: GERARD MANLEY HOPKINS (p. 120)

AIM. To gain some appreciation of the pictures in this poem of pied and dappled things and to feel the intensity which lies behind the poet's expression.

INTRODUCTION. It is an interesting introduction to this poem to get the class to write down a list of pied creatures and objects which attract attention by their colour. Some of these lists may be read out and discussed briefly.

Then read the poem. Read the poem again, for the unusual choice of words and the uncommon construction may not be readily accepted.

DISCUSSION

What does the poet mean by 'couple-colour'?

What two colours do we see in the sky sometimes?

What is the meaning of 'fresh-firecoal chestnut-falls'? The chestnuts which fall in the autumn split open to show the vivid colouring likened to coal freshly on fire.

What would the poet find attractive in the 'gear and tackle and trim' of all trades? Tools with wooden handles and steel blades that not only fit their purpose but are pleasing to look at.

What words in the poem suggest contrast? 'Dappled', 'couple-colour', 'brinded', 'rose-moles', 'stipple', 'counter', 'freckled'.

What words placed together are in strong contrast? Fallow, plough; swift, slow; sweet, sour; adazzle, dim.

What is the feeling of the poet towards all pied beauty? He gives praise to God for all such things and praises God 'whose beauty is past change' for beauty that changes, i.e. 'fickle' or 'adazzle'.

When the poem has been discussed in a way as suggested above, read it through again bringing out clearly the two features which Hopkins revived from Anglo-Saxon verse: alliteration and stress:

> Glóry be to Gód for dáppled thíngs—
> For skíes of cóuple-cólour as a brínded ców;
> For róse-moles all in stípple upon tróut that swím;
> Frésh-fírecoal chéstnut fálls; fínches' wíngs.

INVERSNAID: GERARD MANLEY HOPKINS (p. 120)

AIM. In spite of the difficulties of language to appreciate the vivid images in this poem.

INTRODUCTION. Read the poem to the class explaining briefly that the poet is praising something unusual, wet wildernesses. Read the poem a second time and ask for general comments on first impressions. Many of the images are so original that they will not be immediately understood and may not be accepted until they are explained in some detail. The same comment applies to some of the words which the poet coins for his own use.

DISCUSSION. The difficulties in the poem are of two kinds, one, that of vocabulary, the other, of unusual imagery.

'Horseback brown' is a vivid image of the brown water of the highland stream flowing swiftly down its rocky bed. 'Coop' means 'water cooped up' and 'comb' means 'water combing freely over stones'. The word 'flute' suggests the shape (as in a fluted vase) of the water forming a lip as it flows over the edge of the rock. 'Fleece of his foam' is immediately successful—foam on a stream's surface looking very like fluffs of fleece. The same idea is expressed in 'A windpuff-bonnet of fáwn-fróth'. The word 'twindles' is a composite word, an invention from two words.

The water, like broth in a cauldron, is swirling round in a pool, turning and twisting and suddenly dwindling as it grows less, there is the word 'twindles' a combination of 'twist' and 'dwindles'. 'Degged' means 'sprinkled'. 'Groins' are hollows; 'braes' are hillsides. 'Heathpacks' comes from 'heath', heather. 'Flitches of fern' are ragged tufts.

'The beadbonny ash that sits over the burn' is the poet's way of describing the mountain ash standing beside the stream. The ash has bright red berries which resemble pretty beads. Bonny is Scottish for pretty, and 'beadbonny ash' besides its pleasing sound has concentration of imagery.

After these words have been explained and the imagery discussed, read the poem again to show the force of both imagery and sound.

THE THRUSH'S NEST: JOHN CLARE (p. 121)

AIM. To appreciate the vivid word pictures in this poem, and feel the poet's pleasure in the season.

INTRODUCTION. Read the poem to the class. Read the poem again, asking the class to try to visualize the different pictures presented in the poem.

DISCUSSION

How does the poet show the passing of time in this poem? First he hears the song of the thrush 'from morn to morn'. Then he watches the building of the nest 'from day to day'. Later, 'by and by', he sees the shining eggs 'as bright as flowers'. And, finally, he witnesses 'in the sunny hours' the brood of baby thrushes 'Nature's minstrels chirp and fly'.

What words and phrases show that the poet was happy in what he described?

'A *merry* thrush',
'I drank the sound *with joy*',
'There lay her shining eggs, as *bright as flowers*',
'A brood of Nature's minstrels chirp and fly,
   Glad as the sunshine and the *laughing* sky.'

What words help us to visualize the hawthorn bush? 'Thick and spreading'—and the picture is made more vivid by the second line:

   'That overhung a molehill large and round.'

We can see the soft brown mound and the hawthorn bush bending over it.

'Sing hymns to sunrise.' *Why is this such a good expression?* Hymns suggest adoration of the rising sun.

Does 'I *drank* the sound' *mean more than* 'I *listened to* the sound'? It suggests 'absorbed the sound completely, so that it became a part of him, filling him with joy, a physical sensation'.

What is meant by the phrase, 'intruding guest'? Not invited; he must watch very quietly to see 'the *secret* toil' as the thrush builds the nest.

What unusual word is used to describe the building of the nest?
Warped; here it means 'shaped', a word supported in the next
line by 'modelled'.

Consider carefully the phrases used to describe the thrush's eggs.
Which do you think the most effective? Notice how the description
of the eggs becomes more and more exact. First they are likened
to 'heath-bells gilt with dew'—which is highly poetic, then they
are described 'as bright as flowers'—a vague image though it gives
delicacy to the description; the next line

'Ink-spotted-over shells of greeny blue'

is vivid and exact; we see them clearly now, enhanced by the previous
images.

In what ways is this poem more than a description of a thrush's nest?
It is full of the gladness and wonder of spring. The poet rejoices
in the song of the thrush, the 'sunny hours', and the 'laughing sky'.
It is a poem of joy.

Read the poem again.

THE PIKE: EDMUND BLUNDEN (p. 130)

AIM. To appreciate the vivid pictorial qualities of the poem, and to
illustrate some of the scenes described.

PREPARATION. This is an exciting poem. It contains a number of
difficult words and words used in an unusual context. Some preparation beforehand will lead to a fuller response when the poem is
read.

The following words may be introduced into vocabulary work
some short time before the poem is taken.

bastion: the projecting part of a fortification.

dipper: the water ouzel, acquired its name from its habit of bobbing
up and down.

elver: young eel.

vole: a kind of water-rat.

patriarch: the father and ruler of a family or tribe.

plash: sound of the bulrush striking the water.

vassals: humble servants; slaves.

glutted: gorged with food.

gorgon: one of three mythical sisters whose look turned the beholder to stone; a terrifying creature.

INTRODUCTION. Read the poem to the class, which should more easily visualize the scene, and should recognize roach, bream, ruffe and chub as the names of different varieties of fish.

DISCUSSION

What words describe the scene most vividly?

What sounds disturb 'the broad pool's hush'?

What phrases describe the silent menace of the pike?

> 'still as the dead
> The great pike lies'
> '...now
> Still as a sunken bough.'

What words prepare us for the attack made by the pike?

> '...and quivering poises for slaughter.'

What image is called up by the words 'in fury he lances'?

ILLUSTRATION. Draw or paint any of the scenes described here which appeal to you.

SECTION 3

BALLADS OLD AND NEW

SIR PATRICK SPENS (p. 142)

AIM. By dramatic presentation to try to bring out the tragic force of this narrative poem.

INTRODUCTION. Read the poem to the class.

Read the poem again briefly explaining the unusual words:

braid: plain.   *twine:* sacking.
gane: suffices.   *wap:* pack.
half-fou: half-bushel.   *laith:* loath.
lift: sky.   *aboon:* above.
gurly: rough.   *flattered:* floated.
lap: cracked, sprang.   *gowd kaims:* golden combs.
claith: cloth.   *half-owre:* half-way over.

DISCUSSION. By question and answer build up the story told in the ballad.

The king asks for a good sailor to sail his ship. 'An eldern knight' praises Sir Patrick Spens as the best sailor 'that ever sailed the sea'. Sir Patrick laughs at the idea of sailing at this time of the year, and wonders who has told the king of his name. Is this an act of treachery? However, he has to go:

> 'The king's daughter o' Noroway
> 'Tis thou maun bring her hame.'

They make the journey safely but have not been there a week before Sir Patrick quarrels with the lords of Norway because they said the Scottish men spent all

> 'our king's goud,
> And a' our queenis fee.'

In anger Sir Patrick prepares to sail home, though he is warned of a 'deadly storm'. The story ends tragically, the ship sinks and all on

54

board are drowned, while wives and sweethearts in their finery wait to welcome the voyagers who are lying 'fifty fathoms deep'.

When considering the way in which the story is told in this famous ballad some comparison with the art of the film may be made. The scene is stated in the first two lines

'The king sits in Dunfermline town
Drinking the blude-red wine'

as the scene is set in the opening shots of a film. The dialogue, as in a film, is economical and dramatic.

'O whare will I get a gude sailor
To sail this ship o' mine?'

In a few words the situation is developed; the eldern knight, a favourite of the king, gives the name of Sir Patrick Spens. Immediately a letter is written and sent. Sir Patrick

'Was walking on the strand.'

His reactions are given as in a close-up in the films. In a few words we know that he suspects an act of treachery, that he doesn't want to sail, that he must go. The journey is not described. We are at once in Norway with the speed of the cutting from one place to another in the films. We can tell just what had happened during the Scotsmen's stay in Norway by the dialogue—the quarrel is dramatically presented, again with the economy of the films. Notice the vivid use of detail—'white monie', 'gude red goud'.

Sir Patrick in a moment of rash anger cries:

'Make ready, make ready, my merry men a'!'

His men in consternation warn him of the chance of a 'deadly storm'. The shot in a film would show the same kind of image— a stormy sky—

'I saw the new moon, late yestreen,
Wi' the auld moon in her arm.'

Immediately the story strides forward, and already they are three miles out to sea. Then comes the storm and the shipwreck. How well this could be presented on the films—'the web o' the silken claith' used unavailingly to keep out the incoming sea, and the 'sacking' used in desperation. The Scottish lords so loath to wet their 'cork-heeled shoes'—the feather-beds floating off the deck of the ship. And then the scene shifts to the maidens with gold combs in their hair waiting for the ship's return.

> 'And there lies gude Sir Patrick Spens
> Wi' the Scots lords at his feet.'

CHORAL READING. Single voices: King, the Knight, Sir Patrick Spens, a sailor.

A small group: the Norwegian lords.

Two larger groups.

The narrative should be made subordinate to the actual speeches of the characters in the poem.

One group to alternate with the other in reading the narrative verses.

The last three verses should be spoken quietly by a group of ten voices taken from one of the main groups.

THE WIFE OF USHER'S WELL (p. 145)

AIM. To gain some appreciation of the eerie qualities of this ballad and to consider the effectiveness of the way in which the story is told.

INTRODUCTION. Read the poem to the class, bringing out the matter-of-fact way in which the story is told. This enhances the mysterious, ghostly happening described. Ask for general comments on first impressions. Certain words should be briefly explained before the poem receives further consideration.

wife: woman.	*birk:* birch.
carline: old.	*syke:* marsh.
fashes: troubles, disturbances.	*sheugh:* trench.
Martinmas: 11 November.	*channerin':* fretting.

Read the poem again.

DISCUSSION. Ballad poetry is remarkable for its economy and directness. In three verses the tragic story is told, without comment, without the expression of sympathy for the 'wife of Usher's well'. She was wealthy, she had three sons, she sent them abroad; one week after they had gone she heard that they were dead. Within three weeks the tragic news was confirmed. There is a mounting tension in these three verses, reaching its climax in the fourth verse with the mother's curse:

> 'I wish the wind may never cease,
>   Nor fashes in the flood,
> Till my three sons come hame to me,
>   In earthly flesh and blood!'

Her curse to wind and flood suggests her sons were drowned.

With the greatest economy we are prepared for the ghostly return of her three sons:

> 'In earthly flesh and blood!'

It is November, the nights are 'lang and mirk' suggesting that now anything might happen. The sons return with hats made of the bark of birch, but of birchwood never seen on earth; and we know they are ghosts.

> 'But at the gates o' Paradise,
>   That birk grew fair eneugh.'

The mother in sudden joy thinks her sons who have returned 'are well'. We are reminded that she is a 'wealthy wife' in the orders she gives her maids for the preparations for a feast. As her sons will be tired after their journey she sees them to bed and with her mantle about her she sits 'down at the bedside' like any other affectionate mother would do. After this happy domestic detail comes the warning cock-crow, day is dawning when all spirits must return to the spirit world. The brothers are torn between fear if they delay their departure and concern for their mother who is to suffer another tragic shock:

> 'Gin my mother should miss us when she wakes,
>   She'll go mad ere it be day.'

But they have to leave and the story ends with their sorrowing farewells.

DRAMATIC PRESENTATION. The following speakers should be chosen: A narrator, the carline wife, the eldest son, the youngest son.

The narrator must speak clearly and in a matter-of-fact tone, without striving for any 'ghostly' effects.

The carline wife must show her feelings in her cursing in the fourth verse; and must speak with great vigour and joyfulness in the verse beginning:

'Blow up the fire, my maidens!'

The eldest son should have the heavier voice in contrast to the youngest son who replies

'Brother, we must awa''

and continues in the next verse:

'The cock doth craw, the day doth daw,
    The channerin' worm doth chide;
Gin we be miss'd out o' our place,
    A sair pain we maun bide.'

He feels that they must not delay and urges his brothers to leave at once. The eldest son, thinking of his mother's grief (perhaps he is the favourite son) begs to remain a little longer. Then he realizes that they must go, and sorrowfully speaks the last verse, saying goodbye to his mother, and to the girl

'That kindles my mother's fire!'

THE TWA CORBIES (p. 147)

AIM. To appreciate the economy and force with which the story is told.

INTRODUCTION. Read the poem to the class. Consider the poem carefully before reading it. It attacks suddenly, taking the reader right into the story as so many great poems do. Then two ravens begin their dialogue. A 'mane' is a complaint made because of their hunger; they have no feeling whatsoever for the dead knight. He lies in a sordid place 'yon auld fail dyke' remote and lonely. We have the sense of pointing to the dyke in the word 'yon', it becomes a reality. The ravens have seen the body—

'And naebody kens that he lies there,
But his hawk, his hound, and his lady fair.'

These three living creatures represent the world in which the knight so lately moved. They stand for the world of knighthood, and for such things as obedience, loyalty, dignity. They have all three deserted him. There is merely the statement, with perhaps a hint of treachery, his lady may have killed him for she has soon taken another mate. No comment, except that now the ravens may easily take their 'dinner sweet'.

The stark reality of the scene is shown in the next verse:

> 'Ye'll sit on his white hause-bane,
> And I'll pike out his bonny blue een.'

The birds of prey peck out the eyes of the dead creature first. These will take a lock of his golden hair to thatch their nest. This is direct and vivid and, like truth, pitiless. Then comes the lament, like a cry, high-pitched; and the knight is remembered, but his white bones lie undiscovered where the wind blows.

There is no sentimentality in the poem, and it should be presented realistically, almost grimly.

Certain words need brief explanation:

fail: turf.   *hause-bane:* collar-bone.   *theek:* thatch.

Read the poem again.

DRAMATIC PRESENTATION. When the poem is pretty well understood it may be read as follows:

Narrator.   As I was walking all alane
           I heard twa corbies making a mane;
           The tane unto the t'other did say

1*st Raven.*   'Where sall we gang and dine to-day?'

2*nd Raven.*   'In behint yon auld fail dyke,
           I wot there lies a new-slain knight;
           And naebody kens that he lies there,
           But his hawk, his hound, and his lady fair.

           'His hound is to the hunting gane,
           His hawk to fetch the wild-fowl hame,
           His lady's ta'en another mate,
           So we may make our dinner sweet.'

1st *Raven*.	'Ye'll sit on his white hause-bane,
	And I'll pike out his bonny blue een:
	Wi' ae lock o' his gowden hair,
	We'll theek our nest when it grows bare.'
The two	'Mony a one for him makes mane,
Ravens	But nane sall ken whare he is gane:
together.	O'er his white banes, when they are bare,
	The wind sall blaw for evermair.'

LORD RANDAL (p. 147)

AIM. To bring out the dramatic intensity of the ballad by choral presentation.

INTRODUCTION. Read the poem to the class. It must be spoken with great intensity, starting fairly quietly in tone and mounting with each verse until the anxiety of the mother becomes tragic certainty that her son is going to die. There is a vivid contrast between the increasing fears of the mother and her determination to find out the truth, and the son's attempt to hide everything from his mother and his gradual weakening and final confession. This contrast must be shown—the increasing emphasis in the mother's questioning and the waning strength in her son's replies. Here is a tragic situation dramatically portrayed. The mother is jealous of her son and possessive. He has been meeting his sweetheart in secret. When his mother first asks him where he has been he replies with a lie, 'to the greenwood'. Her suspicions are immediately aroused for she is of a jealous nature, the relationship is not an easy one. When he says

'I met wi' my true-love'

she asks—

'What did she give you?'

His reply,

'eels fried in a pan',

suggest treachery, for the strong flavour would conceal the taste of poison.

Unable to ask directly what she now so terribly fears she wonders where his hounds are? They too have eaten the eels fried in a pan, and now her son knows concealment is useless and gives the vivid detail in his reply:

'they stretched their legs out and died.'

Then comes the final urgency in the mother's voice:

'O I fear you are poisoned',

and the son's reply:

'O yes, I am poisoned',

a fact he had known and tried to conceal from the beginning when he said:

'I hae been at the greenwood.'

DRAMATIC PRESENTATION. When the tragedy is fully understood, the class may be divided into two groups. Light voices should speak for the mother and heavier voices for Lord Randal.

HERIOT'S FORD: RUDYARD KIPLING (p. 169)

AIM. To show the dramatic force of this short modern ballad.

INTRODUCTION. Read the poem to the class bringing out markedly the contrast between the hurried speech and growing fear of the lord, and the calm, determined, relentless speech of his captors.

More is suggested than said in actual words in this poem. We visualize the situation. The captive knight, bound with cords, on horseback, followed by his captors as they move with the setting sun to a place 'three little leagues away', is soon to die. His captors are avenging the death of their sister who died treacherously and unshriven. The tragic story is told in a few incisive sentences, which lead to the climax in the last verse:

'Then wipe the sweat from brow and cheek.'—
'It runnels forth afresh, my Lord.'
'Uphold me, for the flesh is weak.'—
'You've finished with the flesh, my Lord!'

Read the poem a second time.

DRAMATIC PRESENTATION. Here the scene may be enacted by arranging the speakers at the front of the class as follows:

The person speaking the lines of the captured man should have a central position. He should be surrounded on three sides by his captors, four in number. The captured man must show his fear, his furtiveness and finally his almost complete physical collapse. His captors must be courteous (though 'my Lord' becomes increasingly ironical) and yet tersely controlled in their replies, with a growing bitterness in their voices.

O WHAT IS THAT SOUND: W. H. AUDEN (p. 170)

AIM. To present the ballad dramatically, and appreciate the rising force of the action and the tense atmosphere.

INTRODUCTION. Read the poem to the class.

DISCUSSION. The poem, like so many ballads, does not tell a straightforward story. A great deal is left to the imagination, and this vagueness adds to the uneasy atmosphere. We cannot tell just what is happening and all kinds of fears and doubts arise in our minds.

The man and woman (husband and wife?) are unnamed. The scarlet soldiers are not identified (beyond being the red-coats, and we think of the hunting down of the Jacobites). Though the tension rises throughout, the mystery is not explained at the end.

What is the story of the poem about? One possible interpretation is that a husband has some secret which he has kept from his wife. The coming of the soldiers means far more to him than it does to her. She asks the question

> 'O what is that sound which so thrills the ear
> Down in the valley drumming, drumming?'

He replies in a way to allay any anxiety which she may have. They are 'only the scarlet soldiers' on the 'usual manœuvres'. There is nothing to worry about. When the soldiers, however, leave the road and wheel towards their house she falls on her knees as if to implore them to keep away. She tries to make out that the soldiers must be going anywhere but to their house, to the doctor's, the parson's, the farmer's. She is now getting really frightened: the soldiers obviously want someone.

> 'O is it the parson they want with white hair;
>   Is it the parson, is it, is it?'

Note her quickening fear in the repetition 'is it, is it'. Or it must be the farmer—so cunning. But they are coming to *their* house. Who are these soldiers? Why does the husband wait so long and then get ready to go? We think he must be a traitor, conscious of his treachery he is ready to give himself up. This would explain the last line of the poem

> 'And their eyes are burning.'

DRAMATIC PRESENTATION. Divide the class into two groups, one with lighter voices. This group speaks the first two lines of each verse—taking the part of the wife. The other group, speaking quietly throughout, takes the part of the husband. The whole class speaks the last verse in unison.

The poem may be spoken to the sound of drumming feet representing an army marching. This sound should begin very quietly and gradually increase in volume.

THE POET'S HEART

UPON WESTMINSTER BRIDGE: WILLIAM WORDSWORTH (p. 174)

AIM. To appreciate the poet's mood and his sense of wonder at the beauty of the scene on this summer morning in London.

INTRODUCTION. By way of introduction to the poem read Dorothy Wordsworth's description of the same scene in her *Journal*:

'We left London on Saturday morning at ½ past 5 or 6, the 31st of July. (I have forgot which.) We mounted the Dover coach at Charing Cross. It was a beautiful morning. The city, St Paul's, with the river and a multitude of little boats, made a most beautiful sight as we crossed Westminster Bridge. The houses were not overhung by their cloud of smoke, and they were spread out endlessly, yet the sun shone so brightly, with such a fierce light, that there was even something like the purity of one of nature's own grand spectacles.'

Then read the poem to the class, quietly giving full measure to the pauses after the word, 'majesty', at the end of line 3, and the word, 'air', at the end of line 8.

DISCUSSION. The poet is impressed by the brightness of the scene and the stillness at the early hour of the day. The sky is 'smokeless' and he can see the green fields around the city. He compares the city to the countryside and praises those aspects of the city most like the countryside:

'Never did sun more beautifully steep
   In his first splendour, valley, rock, or hill.'

He is filled with a sense of wonder and delight, and he longs to share this feeling. What he writes is not merely a description of the scene as is Dorothy Wordsworth's account, but a moment of his personal joy, a moment of vision. Wordsworth is trying to make us feel just how he felt at this moment of time. He says:

'The river glideth at his own sweet will'

because that is what he feels about the river just then, and:

'Dear God! the very houses seem asleep'

Wordsworth felt that by saying this we should feel with him. He has created his own private world and we go into it and understand it because of our own world of the imagination.

Read the poem again to bring out the points raised in the discussion.

JERUSALEM: WILLIAM BLAKE (p. 180)

AIM. To try to share the intense religious feeling of the poem, and to appreciate the vivid imagery which expresses the sincerity of the poet.

INTRODUCTION. Read the poem to the class bringing out the intensity of feeling. Read the poem again, and ask the class for general comments on first impressions.

DISCUSSION

How does this poem differ from other lyrical poems? It is religious in feeling and has become a most popular hymn.

What is the effect of the questions in the first two verses? They arrest the attention and force the reader to think of the possibilities the poet suggests.

What gives its power to the third verse? The vivid imagery, reminding one of the imagery of the more inspired parts of the Bible. The poet's desire to build Jerusalem again in 'England's green and pleasant land' is so great that he can only express it by means of symbols—the 'bow of burning gold', the 'arrows of desire', the 'chariot of fire', all closely associated with the impassioned utterances of prophets and seers in the Old Testament.

What examples of the effective use of alliteration occur in the poem?
'pleasant pastures',
'Bring me my bow of burning gold',
'sword sleep',
'In England's green and pleasant land'.

CHORAL READING. Divide the class into two groups.
The first group speaks the first two lines of the first verse.
The second group speaks the next two lines.
The first group speaks the first two lines of the second verse.
The second group speaks the next two lines.
Both groups together speak the third verse.
The first group speaks the first line of the fourth verse.
The second group speaks the second line of the fourth verse.
Both groups together speak the last two lines.
The whole poem to be spoken with intense feeling.

THERE WAS AN INDIAN: J. C. SQUIRE (p. 181)

AIM. To try to appreciate through the power of the imagination the feeling of the Indian when Columbus landed in America.

INTRODUCTION. Read the poem to the class and ask for general comments on first impressions.

What imaginative demand is made on the reader? That he should try to experience the feelings of the Indian when Columbus landed on his shores.

DISCUSSION. Take the class through the poem by asking a series of questions such as the following:

Why had the Indian known no change?

What expression continues the thought given in the first line? 'Strayed content.'

How do we imagine the Indian from the first two and a half lines? Happy; innocent; content 'gathering shells'.

What is the meaning of 'commingled'?

Why does the Indian gasp for speech? Because he sees something he has never seen before and cannot put into words.

Why does the poet describe the ships of Columbus as

'...huge canoes,
With bellying cloths on poles, and not one oar,
And fluttering coloured signs and clambering crews'?

Because he sees them through the eyes of the Indian who knows only canoes, and cloths, poles and oars.

What word shows how bewildered the Indian was by the sight? 'Magic'—he thought the 'canoes' moved on the sea by magic.

What does he call the flags on the ships? 'Fluttering coloured signs.'

What is implied in the word 'knelt' which would be lost if the word 'crouched' were used? Kneeling suggests reverence, the ships came by magic, bringing, perhaps, some new god.

Why are the ships called 'doom-burdened'? This is an impressive word both by meaning and by its heavy sound. It suggests the doom of the Indians who would now lose their happy innocent way of life, and the discovery of America was a turning-point in the history of the world.

Why are the ships called 'caravels'? This is a more romantic word (cf. Keats's 'argosies' in *The Eve of St Agnes*).

What image is called up by the word 'slant' in the last line of the poem? Why is it so effective?

Read the poem again.

ON FIRST LOOKING INTO CHAPMAN'S HOMER: JOHN KEATS (p. 182)

AIM. To appreciate the intense feeling of discovery expressed in this poem, and to compare it with *There was an Indian*.

INTRODUCTION. This poem also deals with a discovery, not the discovery of a continent but of the realm of Homer's poetry. It expresses the excitement the poet felt when he first read Chapman's translation of Homer.

Read the poem. Read the poem again, asking the class to notice particularly the comparisons made.

DISCUSSION

What are 'the realms of gold'? The world of poetry.

How is the idea of 'realms' for literature continued in the poem? In the phrases 'goodly states', 'kingdoms', 'western islands', 'wide expanse', 'demesne'.

What is meant by 'western islands'? The whole of English poetry.
Explain 'Which bards in fealty to Apollo hold'. Which poets
hold in allegiance to the Greek god, Apollo, who was not only the
god of the sun but also of literature.

Why 'deep-browed Homer'? Homer was blind, and a famous piece
of sculpture shows him bending over the lyre with wrinkled brow
to show his concentration.

'Yet did I never breathe its pure serene.'

Explain the meaning of this line. Keats was unable to read Greek,
and could not enjoy the wonders of Homer's poetry until he read
the translation made by George Chapman, an Elizabethan poet.

Why 'loud and bold'? Because Chapman's translation has the
vigour and directness of Elizabethan literature.

There are two wonderful comparisons in the poem: one to the
discovery of a new planet, the other to the discovery of the Pacific.
You can feel the thrill in the lines:

'Then felt I like some watcher of the skies
When a new planet swims into his ken.'

Which word strikes you as most unusual here? The word 'swims',
which gives an unforgettable image.

*What must the feelings of the first white man to see the Pacific,
a new, unknown ocean, have been?* Though it is believed to have been
Balboa, Keats names Cortez, another Spanish explorer.

Consider carefully the excitement and wonder in these last four
lines.

Why 'stout Cortez'? 'Stout' means brave, resolute; together the
two words have a ringing sound, the splendid image is enriched by
the phrase 'with eagle eyes'.

The sense of wonder is caught in the lines

'He stared at the Pacific—and all his men
Looked at each other with a wild surmise—
Silent, upon a peak in Darien.'

What was their wild surmise? A hesitation to believe that what
they were staring at could indeed be a new ocean.

Why were they silent? They were lost in awe because no words could be adequate to describe how they felt, and what they saw.

Notice the perfect ending to this poem, the superb distribution of sound in the last line with the pause after 'silent' and the stress falling in such a way as to leave echoes in the mind

'Sílent, upon a péak in Dárien.'

COMPARISON BETWEEN THE TWO POEMS. In *There was an Indian*, the poet describes a single incident; he does this simply and objectively.

Keats describes an experience which has moved him deeply. To express what he has experienced he uses heightened language, metaphors and similes which fit perfectly into the poem and make it a complete unity and completely satisfying. His choice of words is both more original and more poetic.

PART III

THE MAGIC OF WORDS

ROMANCE: W. J. TURNER (p. 5)

AIM. To feel something of the magic of the words which give this poem its title, *Romance*.

INTRODUCTION. Read the poem paying particular attention to the words Chimborazo, Cotopaxi, and Popocatapetl.

DISCUSSION

What is the theme of the poem? The magic that lies in romantic proper names. Here the sound and associations of the names Chimborazo, Cotopaxi and Popocatapetl have captured the imagination of the boy, when 'but thirteen or so'.

What lines in the poem tell us of the change which has come over the boy?

'I went into a golden land.'
'My father died, my brother too,
    They passed like fleeting dreams.'
'I dimly heard the Master's voice
    And boys far-off at play.'
'I walked in a great golden dream
    To and fro from school.'
'I walked home with a gold dark boy
    And never a word I'd say.'
'The houses, people, traffic seemed
    Thin fading dreams by day.'

Why is the word 'golden' or 'gold' used in this poem? Because of its romantic associations with distant countries, and it suggests also the glowing light in the boy's imagination.

CHORAL READING. Divide the class into two groups.
    Group I to speak the first two lines of each verse.

73

Group II to speak the next two lines, enunciating the proper names clearly as the success of the reading depends very largely on these three words.

EPILOGUE TO 'HASSAN': JAMES ELROY FLECKER (p. 9)

AIM. To enjoy the rich romantic qualities of the verse by choral speaking.

INTRODUCTION. Explain briefly that Hassan and Ishak, hating the tyrannical rule of the Caliph of Bagdad, decide to disguise themselves as pilgrims and travel with a caravan to Samarkand.

The scene is at the Gate of the Sun in Bagdad. It is a moonlit night. By the gate stands the Watchman with a great key. The crowd in front of him consists of merchants, camel-drivers, pilgrims, Jews, women. Among the pilgrims Hassan and Ishak are waiting to leave the city.

A few words and phrases need explanation:

spikenard: an aromatic substance from an Eastern plant.
mastic: a kind of resin.
terebinth: a turpentine-yielding tree.
God's Own Prophet: Mahomet.
manuscripts in peacock styles: illuminated in gorgeous colours.

CHORAL SPEAKING. Eastern people usually sit with their legs crossed like tailors. Make up the various groups either sitting in this way or standing. We want groups as follows:

The Merchants, The Principal Jews, a small group to speak the lines of the Chief Draper and another to speak for the Chief Grocer. Single voices speak the lines of the Master of the Caravan, Principal Jew, the Chief Merchant, One of the Women, an Old Man, Hassan, Ishak, the Watchman.

The refrain, 'We take the Golden Road to Samarkand', must be repeated with increasing excitement because it is the keynote to the whole scene.

CARGOES: JOHN MASEFIELD (p. 12)

AIM. To appreciate the flavour and the associations of the words in this poem.

INTRODUCTION. Read the poem through. Read the poem again and ask for general impressions.

DISCUSSION. The effectiveness of this poem depends very largely upon the sound and associations of the words. Each stanza presents a complete picture.

STANZA I

What effect is achieved in this stanza? The stateliness of the rhythm and the particular choice of words suggest the opulence and elegance of the East.

Quinquireme is a galley with five banks of oars.

Nineveh is an antique city of fabled wealth.

Ophir is the place from which Solomon is said to have brought his gold.

Haven is a more romantic word than harbour.

The cargo consists of luxurious, elegant, exotic things: ivory, apes, peacocks (all bringing to mind something rich and fantastic). Sandalwood suggests sweet scents, cedarwood by association brings thoughts of the Cedars of Lebanon, the building of the Temple, incense and worship.

What are the different appeals to the senses?

Ivory, smooth and polished, appeals to the sense of touch.

Apes and peacocks, rare fantastic creatures, to the sense of sight.

Sandalwood and cedarwood to the sense of smell.

Sweet white wine to the sense of taste.

STANZA II

The rhythm of this stanza is also stately in movement.

What is the effect achieved here? The wealth of the Indies. The Spanish galleon is coming from the Isthmus of Panama. Here the

75

cargo consists of precious stones, spices and gold coin. (Notice the romantic names: amethysts, topazes, cinnamon and moidores.)

The first two stanzas are rich in romantic, high-sounding words and are shot through by colour and sunshine.

STANZA III

In what ways is this stanza in strong contrast with the first two? There is a marked change in rhythm with the lines full of harsh-sounding consonants. Compare the following lines for sound:

Quinquireme of Nineveh from distant Ophir

and

Dirty British coaster with a salt-caked smoke stack.

The first line moves smoothly and without effort, the other is spoken with harsh laboured emphasis, suggesting the laboured progress of the ship, a progress sharply expressed in the word 'butting'.

The cargo of the coaster is severely practical and ugly: coal, metal, and firewood. This ugliness, standing as a comment on an industrial age heightens the grace and beauty described in the first two stanzas.

The words in the last stanza have been chosen with just as much care to achieve a different effect from the rest of the poem. They are harsh staccato words: 'salt-caked', 'smoke stack' (for the softer sounding 'funnel'), 'butting' for 'steaming', 'road-rails', 'pig-lead', and the final thin rattling phrase 'cheap tin trays'.

Read the poem again to bring out the various aspects of the poem mentioned in the discussion.

LEPANTO: G. K. CHESTERTON (p. 12)

AIM. To enjoy the vigour of the verse and the flavour of romantic names by choral reading.

INTRODUCTION. Lepanto was a naval battle fought in 1571 in the Gulf of Corinth between the Turks and the forces of the Christian League. These forces came from Spain, Austria, Venice, Genoa, Sicily and Naples and were inspired by Pope Pius V. Don John of

Austria won a great victory, and saved Europe from the Turks and Christianity from Islam. In Don John's army fought Cervantes, the author of *Don Quixote*. In this romantic story Don Quixote might be described as 'the last knight of Europe'.

CHORAL READING. Divide the class into two groups:
    Group I speaks the opening lines of the poem from:

        'White founts falling in the Courts of the sun'
down to:
'And called the kings of Christendom for swords about the Cross.'

    A single voice to speak the next two lines:

        'The cold queen of England is looking in the glass;
        The shadow of the Valois is yawning at the Mass.'

Group I speaks the next two lines.
Group II speaks the next section of the poem from

        'Dim drums throbbing, in the hills half heard...'
down to:
        'Spurning of his stirrups like the thrones of all the world.'

Groups I and II together speak the next five lines.
Group I speaks the next section from:

        'Mahound is in his paradise above the evening star...'
down to:
        'When Solomon was king.'

The line in italics and brackets (*Don John of Austria is going to the war*) is said in unison, here and throughout the poem.
Group II speaks the next section from:

'They rush in red and purple from the red clouds of the morn'
down to:
'Put down your feet upon him, that our peace be on the earth.'

The combined groups speak the next six lines.

Group I speaks the next section from:

'St Michael's on his Mountain in the sea-roads of the north' down to:

'But Don John of Austria is riding to the sea.'

Both groups together speak the next six lines.
A single voice speaks the lines:

'King Philip's in his closet with the Fleece about his neck'

down to:

'But Don John of Austria has fired upon the Turk.'

Both groups speak the next six lines.
Group II speaks the next section beginning:

'The Pope was in his chapel before day or battle broke'

down to:

'And he finds his God forgotten, and he seeks no more a sign—'

Both groups speak the next eleven lines down to:

'Has set his people free!'

A single voice speaks the last section:

'Cervantes on his galley sets the sword back in the sheath'

down to:

'And he smiles, but not as Sultans smile, and settles back the
   blade...'.

The lines in italics are spoken in unison.

TARANTELLA: HILAIRE BELLOC (p. 19)

AIM. To enjoy by choral speaking the lively dance measure of this
poem.

INTRODUCTION. Mr A. S. T. Fisher in his *Voice and Verse*, Part II,
has the following interesting note on this poem:

'In the country round the port of Taranto in the heel of Italy is
a spider, the "Tarantula", whose bite was supposed to be very
poisonous. The remedy was for the patient to fling himself into a
very lively dance and Pepys notes in his Diary a traveller's report

that, at harvest time when the spiders are most active, "fiddlers go up and down the fields in expectation of being hired by those that are stung". Such a dance was known as a Tarantella.'

Read the poem, keeping the measure of the lively rapid dance throughout the first section. The last lines of the poem are spoken more slowly than the rest.

CHORAL SPEAKING. This poem gives opportunity for practice in very lively alert speaking. It is full of pleasant sounds, the imitation of the music of castanets and guitar:

> 'Snapping of the clapper to the spin
> Out and in—
> And the Ting, Tong, Tang of the guitar'

and the spinning dancing movement of the first part:

> 'And the cheers and the jeers of the young muleteers
> Who hadn't got a penny,
> And who weren't paying any,
> And the hammer at the doors and the Din?'

This is in strong contrast to the last section of the poem with the long vowel sounds and the consonants 'm', 'n', and 'd' giving a heavy, sad movement.

> 'Never more;
> Miranda,
> Never more....'

Divide the class into two groups, Group I with light voices, Group II with heavier voices. Group I speaks the first part, and Group II the second part, of the poem.

THE POET'S VISION

TO AUTUMN: JOHN KEATS (p. 30)

AIM. To try to visualize clearly the pictures of autumn, to realize the other appeals to the senses, and appreciate the suggestive power of the poem.

INTRODUCTION. Read the letter from Keats to his friend Reynolds, written from Winchester, 22 September 1819. (The Ode was written on 19 September.)

'How beautiful the season is now.—How fine the air—a temperate sharpness about. Really, without joking, chaste weather. Dian skies—I never liked a stubble field so much as now.—Aye better than the chilly green of the Spring. Somehow a stubble field looks warm—in the same way that some pictures look warm. This struck me so much in my Sunday's walk that I composed upon it.'

Read the poem. Read the poem again asking the class to consider carefully the theme of each stanza.

DISCUSSION
What is the general theme of each stanza?
STANZA I. The fruitfulness of autumn.
STANZA II. The occupations of autumn.
STANZA III. The sounds and colours of autumn.

STANZA I

What is the theme, and how is it developed? The fruitfulness of autumn:

  (i) The maturing ripeness of the season, the continuing warmth of the sun.
  (ii) The fruits: the vines, apples, hazel-nuts.
  (iii) The flowers and honey.

What pictures are presented? Autumn is personified as a bosom-friend of the sun and they are conspiring together.

'The vines that round the thatch-eaves run.'

'The moss'd cottage-trees' (a wonderfully concentrated picture).

'To plump the hazel shells' (one can almost feel the shape of the hazel nuts after the word, 'plump').

'O'er-brimm'd their clammy cells.' (Notice how these lines suggest the buzzing of the bees on a warm drowsy autumn day.)

STANZA II

What occupations of autumn are mentioned?

That of a 'winnower in the barn'.

A reaper asleep in the field.

A gleaner crossing a brook.

A worker watching by a cider-press.

What is the value of personification? It presents an abstraction as a living object, gaining in concrete reality; it also gains in concentration.

What phrases suggest the mellow warmth of autumn?

> '...sound asleep,
> Drows'd with the fume of poppies.'

> '...with patient look,
> Thou watchest the last oozings, hours by hours.'

What sounds suggest the actions they describe?

> '...like a gleaner thou dost keep
> Steady thy laden head across a brook.'

Here there is a slight pause after the word 'keep' and one steps from one line to the next on the word 'Steady' almost as though one were the gleaner crossing the brook.

> '...watchest the last oozings, hours by hours.'

Here the long vowel sounds suggest the slow dripping of the cider from the press and the slow passing of time.

STANZA III

The theme is the sounds and colours of autumn.
What sounds are described?

'A wailful choir the small gnats mourn.'
'Full-grown lambs loud bleat from hilly bourn.'
'Hedge-crickets sing.'
'The red-breast whistles from a garden-croft.'
'Gathering swallows twitter in the skies.'

What do you notice about these sounds? They are all thin sounds,
as if they were in key with the passing of the year: wailful choir,
loud bleat, hedge-crickets sing, whistles, twitter.
What colours are suggested?

'...barrèd clouds bloom the soft-dying day' (the pink
of cirrus clouds at sunset).

'...touch the stubble-plains with rosy hue.'

The pink glow on the warm earth of the harvest fields. Notice the
unromantic associations of 'stubble-plains'.
How do the sounds and the imagery suit the subject? The poet is
describing the beauty of the season. The sounds and the images used
at the beginning of this stanza give the warm rosy glow of a perfect
autumn day. Then he describes the wailful choir of the gnats, the
bleat of full-grown lambs, the whistle of the robin (reminding us of
the approach of winter), the gathering swallows (soon to depart)
and autumn will be over. It is rather like a full symphony of sound
gradually reducing in volume until the violins alone fade into silence

'...twitter in the skies.'

swath is the band of corn to be cut with the next sweep of the sickle.
sallow: a kind of willow.
full-grown lambs: because they were born in the early spring.
bourn means boundary or limit. Here the word is used to mean
'region'.

Read the poem through again.

ODE TO THE WEST WIND: P. B. SHELLEY (p. 35)

AIM. To appreciate the vivid pictures presented in this poem, and to consider carefully the use of personification.

INTRODUCTION. Read the poem to the class. Read the poem again, asking for general comments on first impressions.

DISCUSSION. This poem is not an easy one because of the richness of the crowded images. But the plan on which the poem is composed should readily be seen.

What is the theme of each of the first three stanzas? The first stanza describes the wind blowing the leaves like 'pestilence-stricken multitudes'. The second stanza describes the wind blowing the clouds like 'earth's decaying leaves'. The third stanza describes how the waves of the blue Mediterranean are wakened by the wind.

How does the fourth stanza recall the theme of each of the previous stanzas? In the first three lines the poet refers to a leaf, a cloud and a wave each in the power of the wind. These three words, 'wave', 'leaf', and 'cloud' are used again in the eleventh line of this stanza.

What is the theme of the last stanza? The desire of the poet to be inspired by the spirit of the west wind.

STANZA I

What examples of the use of personification and simile are there in this stanza? The wind is a living thing, though unseen, driving the dead leaves and the winged seeds before it. It is a Destroyer and Preserver. Spring is the 'azure sister' blowing a trumpet to waken the Earth. The leaves are driven like ghosts, they are a pestilence-stricken multitude. The seeds are like corpses. The sweet buds are driven like flocks to feed in air.

STANZA II

Which do you consider the most effective image in this stanza? Notice how the poet writes about the great elemental forces of nature: the 'sky's commotion', 'loose clouds', 'boughs of heaven

83   6-2

and ocean', 'Angels of rain and lightning', 'airy surge'. This is in strong contrast to the striking simile:

> 'Like the bright hair uplifted from the head
> Of some fierce Maenad.'

STANZA III

What use is made of personification here? The Mediterranean is personified as a man asleep in the summer dreaming of 'old palaces and towers'

> 'Quivering within the wave's intenser day.'

He is wakened gently from his dreams, for the wind is not so violent here as when it cleaves the Atlantic, frightening the very seaweed in the depths.

STANZA IV

What desires of the poet are expressed here? He wishes to share the strength and the uncontrollable movement of the wind. He feels 'chained and bowed' and wants to enjoy the freedom of the wind.

STANZA V

In what ways does this stanza remind us of the first one? The poet likens his thoughts to withered leaves which should be driven 'over the universe' (like the withered leaves in the first stanza) to quicken a new birth like the seeds which 'lie cold and low' and then in the spring fill

> 'With living hues and odours plain and hill.'

So the 'incantation of this verse' will be to unawakened earth

> 'The trumpet of a prophecy',

for he will show as does the wind, that

> 'If Winter comes, can Spring be far behind?'

However dark life may be, he can prophesy a new hope, a better world.

THE CLOUD: P. B. SHELLEY (p. 38)

AIM. To appreciate the elaborate imagery and the swift lyrical movement of the verse.

INTRODUCTION. Read the poem to the class. The first reading should be fairly slow on account of the elaborate imagery. Read the poem again more quickly to show the smooth movement of the verse.

DISCUSSION. The brilliance and variety of the imagery are understood more fully if the thought of the poem is given briefly. The Cloud is telling its own story. It has many different forms and many different moods.

STANZA I

The Cloud is made from the moisture of seas and streams and brings showers to the trees and flowers; it gives shade, appears as hail or rain or thunder.

STANZA II

It can bring snow, be blown across the sky charged with lightning and thunder; part of the cloud is bathed in sunshine from above and dissolving in showers beneath.

STANZA III

The sunrise can light up the cloud, just as an eagle on a crag can be illumined by the sunshine. Or the cloud can move gently on a peaceful evening

'As still as a brooding dove.'

STANZA IV

The moon glides over the fleece-like floor of the cloud, and where there are holes in the layers of cloud the stars peep through. As the cloud moves the holes get larger, the rivers, lakes and seas can be seen reflecting the moon and the stars as if the sky had fallen through the holes in the cloud.

85

STANZA V

The cloud then obscures the sun and screens the moon; then it is carried along by the whirlwinds, and covers the whole of the sky 'like a roof'. This is the triumphal arch of the cloud decorated by the wide spanning rainbow.

STANZA VI

The cloud is made of air and water, it changes but cannot die. After it dissolves completely in rain, winds and sunshine rebuild the 'blue dome of air' and the cloud appears out of the caverns of rain

'...like a ghost from the tomb'

and unbuilds that blue dome of air. The cloud has appeared again in the blue sky.

What images are most effective and why?

Note the accuracy of the imagery in relation to the scientific facts.

What is the effect of the internal rhymes?

'I bring fresh *showers* for the thirsting *flowers*.'

The verse, like the subject, is swift-moving, light and delicate, due very largely to the skilful use of the internal rhymes and a subtle use of vowel sounds.

THE ICE-CART: W. W. GIBSON (p. 41)

AIM. To appreciate the pictorial qualities of this poem.

INTRODUCTION. Read the poem. Read the poem again asking the class to notice particularly the imagery.

DISCUSSION. This is a poem of contrasts.

What is contrasted? The close, stuffy office, the grey and grimy heat of 'that intolerable street' and the clean cold of Polar regions.

Why does the clerk watch the carter 'with envy'? Because the carter is handling ice on a stifling hot day.

Why is the street called 'intolerable'? Because it is drab, depressing and airless in the heat.

What leads the clerk to day-dream about Polar regions? The sight of the carter handling ice.

What words describe the colours of the Polar scene? Sapphire, emerald, ruby.

What do you notice about these words? They are all the names of precious stones.

Why are these names used instead of blue, green and red? Because they are more unusual, more arresting; and precious stones are crystalline like ice and shine so that we get a more exact picture in our mind's eye.

Where is the description of 'shining' objects continued? In the description of the 'shining' seals, the seas of 'blinding' blue.

The clerk dreams not only of the refreshing coldness of the Polar regions but of action, in contrast to his own inaction on the office stool.

What violent actions are described in his dream? The bears 'plunged headlong down with flourished heels'. They floundered after 'shining seals'. Then he too is swimming among the seal-pack

> 'thrusting on with threshing tail',
> 'twist and twirl and sudden leap',
> 'Diving and doubling with my kind.'

All these phrases describe violent physical action.

What change do you notice after the description of this violent action? He dreams about rest and sleep.

How is this described? By the use of gentle soft-sounding words

> 'Snow drifting gently fine and white...',
> 'Beneath that cold white drifting sleep—
> Sleep drifting deep,
> Deep drifting sleep....'

How do we know that it is all a dream? By the words 'drifting sleep—sleep drifting deep'.

At what point does the clerk wake up? When the carter suddenly cracks his whip.

What words show how the clerk is jerked out of his sleep? He 'clutched' his stool with 'startled grip'.

What do you notice about the last two lines in the poem? They repeat what is said at the beginning, and recall the clerk to the reality of his everyday life.

Read the poem through again.

WINTER THE HUNTSMAN: OSBERT SITWELL (p. 43)

AIM. To appreciate the carefully worked out analogy in this poem.

INTRODUCTION. Read the poem through without explanation or comment. Ask for general comments on first impressions. Read the poem again before discussing the general theme of each stanza.

DISCUSSION

STANZA I

What is the theme? That the progress of winter across the country-side is like that of a relentless huntsman.

Why is winter called a Huntsman? Because winter is pitiless like a hunter and brings death to many creatures.

What two aspects of winter are brought out in this stanza? The hardness, 'iron glades', and colourlessness of winter 'all colour fades'.

STANZA II

What is the theme? The violence of winter in storms, with the roaring of the wind and the tearing of branches from the trees.

STANZA III

What is the theme? The fox is described, and the falling leaves. Even the hardy fox, a creature of the wilds, *creeps* to his hole; the fading leaves fall, and the 'bare trees shiver'. 'All colour fades' is true when the fox and the copper leaves have disappeared.

STANZA IV

What is the theme? The increasing desolation of winter. Colour is still fading 'night creeps from the ground', and sound is also dying leaving a desolation.

88

STANZA V

What is the theme? A summing up of the preceding stanzas. The first line:

'Is it Winter the Huntsman'

recalls the first stanza describing winter as a huntsman riding through the iron glades. The second line:

'Who gallops through his iron glades'

continues the thought in the first stanza and with the word, 'gallops' recalls the second stanza with the wild crashing hooves. The third line:

'Cracking his cruel whip'

suggests the cruelty of winter to all living things—as represented by the fox in the third stanza. The fourth line:

'To the gathering shades'

recalls the darkness of night, and the desolate silence of the fourth stanza.

What picture do you form of Winter the Huntsman?

LONDON SNOW: ROBERT BRIDGES (p. 43)

AIM. To show how this poem satisfies 'both eye and ear', and to compare it with *Snow in the Suburbs*.

INTRODUCTION. Read the poem through slowly to give full value to the sound of the words and to allow the images to form in the mind's eye. Read the poem again and ask for general comments on first impressions.

DISCUSSION

How does this description compare with your own experience?

Divide the poem into sections according to the progression of the description.

The poem opens with a description of snow falling, this wonderful description continues down to the ninth line. Then comes a section describing the unusual effect of the snow lying thick in its 'uncompacted lightness'—the 'unaccustomed brightness', the 'strange unheavenly glare', 'the dazzling whiteness', and the strange silence 'the stillness of the solemn air'.

The third section describes boys going to school and their excited actions in the snow; a few carts 'creak and blunder', the sun shines palely and awakes the 'stir of the day'.

The last section describes the 'war waged with the snow', men going to work 'tread long brown paths' and diverted by the beauty of the snow forget their everyday worries for a moment even as they spoil the beauty they mention.

Point out examples of careful observation.

The poem abounds in wonderfully accurate descriptions. Consider the many examples given by the class and try to point out just what makes each one so effective.

What passages appeal to the ear as well as to the eye?

Comment on such passages as the description of the falling snow:

> 'Stealthily and perpetually settling and loosely lying,
>   Hushing the latest traffic of the drowsy town'

with its long vowel sounds suggesting the hushed slow falling of the snow. Notice the drowsy almost hypnotic effect of the sounds in

> 'Lazily and incessantly floating down and down
>   Silently sifting and veiling road, roof and railing.'

We not only see the scene described, we hear the muted sounds and almost feel the snow falling round us.

Other passages to comment on for their sound: the mounting excitement of the school boys:

> 'Or peering up from under the white-mossed wonder,
>   "O look at the trees!" they cried, "O look at the trees!"'

and the phrases such as: 'a few carts creak and *blunder*' (where 'blunder' gives the slight lurch of the cart on the snow).

> 'Tread long brown paths, as toward their toil they go'

(with long vowel sounds, monosyllables suggesting the weary effort of these 'sombre men').

SNOW IN THE SUBURBS: THOMAS HARDY (p. 44)

AIM. To appreciate the visual effects in the poem.

INTRODUCTION. Read the poem to the class without comment. Read the poem again asking the class to pay particular attention to the pictorial qualities.

DISCUSSION. It is obviously an advantage to read this poem in winter after snow has fallen so that the class may compare their own observations with those of the poet. This, however, is not always possible and the class may have to rely on winter scenes remembered.

What indications are there in the first stanza that it has been a heavy fall of snow?

What expressions are particularly vivid?

> 'Every fork like a white web-foot.'

Discuss the pictorial quality of this line with the class.

How do we know that it is still snowing?

> 'Some flakes have lost their way, and grope back upward, when Meeting those meandering down they turn and descend again.'

Show how these lines not only tell us that it is snowing but bring to mind vividly just how snow does fall—drifting through the air. Note 'grope back upward'. Is this a good description? Why? 'Meeting those meandering'—how does this give the impression of the floating snow-flakes?

The 'm' sounds, and the soft sounding word 'meandering'.

Ask for comments on the effectiveness of the word 'glued' in the line: 'The palings are glued together like a wall.'

What is the effect of the alliteration in the last line of this stanza? The use of the 'w's' and 'f's' in 'waft of wind' and 'fleecy fall' is to give the muted sound we experience when snow has fallen.

What is the theme of the second stanza? A sparrow, so much at home in trees, is now confused by the change and is nearly buried in a fall of snow from one of the branches. This fall of snow 'starts off a volley of other lodging lumps with a rush'. Notice the vivid reality of this description, what might appear a trivial incident by the accuracy of presentation becomes important.

Why is the cat in the last stanza 'wide-eyed and thin'? The cat is lost in this suddenly changed world. It can't find food and is utterly miserable 'with feeble hope'. Comfort now lies inside, and so 'we take him in'.

Which picture of the scene presented here do you find the most effective?

COMPARISON

In what ways do these two poems resemble each other, and how do they differ? Both deal with the same subject. Both describe snow falling and snow lying deep. *London Snow* describes snow falling in greater detail; compare the first nine lines of that poem with the two lines of *Snow in the Suburbs*:

'Some flakes have lost their way, and grope back upward, when
Meeting those meandering down they turn and descend again.'

This seems a more personal description. The whole of Hardy's poem is more individual. Bridges is altogether more conventional. We feel that we might have described the scene more as he has done. Hardy uses phrases that are both daring and original, such as 'like a white web-foot', 'palings are glued together like a wall', 'a volley of other lodging lumps'. Compare these with phrases from *London Snow* such as:

'Hushing the latest traffic of the drowsy town'
and
'And all woke earlier for the unaccustomed brightness.'

Both poems give a most effective picture of the scene, and the sound suits the sense.

NARRATIVE POEMS ON SEA AND LAND

THE HIGH TIDE ON THE COAST OF LINCOLNSHIRE, 1571: JEAN INGELOW (p. 50)

AIM. To appreciate the dramatic qualities of the poem and see how the changing movement of the verse suggests mood and atmosphere.

INTRODUCTION. This is a modern narrative poem based on an Elizabethan story, and it retains in spelling and phrasing the spirit of the sixteenth century.

Read the poem to the class.

DISCUSSION

What is the poem about?

Who is telling the story?

What is the old woman doing when the story opens? What can she see? What can she hear? She sees her 'sonne's faire wife, Elizabeth' and hears her milking song.

When did the Boston bells ring 'The Brides of Enderby'? To give warning 'of pyrate galleys warping downe'; 'for shippes ashore beyond the scorpe', for some 'evil news'.

What was the disastrous news brought by the old woman's son?

> 'The olde sea wall (he cried) is downe
> The rising tide comes on apace....'

Why was he so frightened? Because of his anxiety for his wife Elizabeth.

Which lines describe the effect of the tidal wave?

> 'Then bankes came down with ruin and rout,—
> Then beaten foam flew round about,—
> Then all the mighty floods were out.'

93

What happened to Elizabeth and her two children? They were drowned and their bodies

> 'Ere yet the early dawn was clear...
> Downe drifted to thy dwelling-place.'

This poem is full of variety and the movement of the verse shows great power in suggesting mood and atmosphere.

The sense of urgency is given in the opening stanza as the ringers run to pull the bells urged on by the mayor.

There is the suggestion of a strange happening in the lines:

> 'The flight of mews and peewits pied
> By millions crouched on the old sea-wall.'

The incident is seen through the eyes of the old woman, which adds to the dramatic force of the poem. Her recital begins on a quiet domestic note, to heighten the tragedy to come.

> 'I sat and spun within the doore,
> My thread brake off, I raised myne eyes!'

We have Elizabeth's lovely milking song:

> 'Cusha! Cusha! Cusha! calling'

with the descriptions of the meadows,

> 'where the reedy Lindis floweth.'

The pleasant sounding names of the cows—Whitefoot, Lightfoot, Jetty—adds charm to the pastoral scene.

Then comes the anxious warning of the bells, playing 'The Brides of Enderby'. The excitement rises when the old woman's son comes riding down shouting for his wife Elizabeth as the rising tide floods the flat land.

They see the tidal wave, vividly described 'like a curling snow-white cloud', and the poem rushes on to its climax of disaster.

The poem ends most fittingly with the milking song which the old woman would never hear again. Some words and phrases may need explanation before arranging the poem for dramatic reading:

The belfry tower: this is the large tower known as 'Boston Stump'.

Ply all your changes, all your swells: ring your bells in different order and in changing volume of sound.

a stolen tyde: a tide of unusual size.
melick: a kind of grass.
bin: is.
warping downe: approaching.
eygre: tidal wave.
weltering: overflowing.

DRAMATIC PRESENTATION. Single voices to speak for the mayor and the son. The story to be told by a group of about a dozen. The milking song to be spoken by the full chorus.

THE 'REVENGE': LORD TENNYSON (p. 57)

AIM. To give briefly the historical background, and by dramatic presentation gain a fuller appreciation of the vigour and poetic force of this poem.

INTRODUCTION. First give a brief account of the historical event on which the poem is based.

In 1591, Lord Thomas Howard had been sent with a small fleet of men-o'-war to the Azores to intercept a Spanish treasure-fleet. He did not expect to find a large number of warships acting as convoy to this treasure fleet. He was outnumbered, many of his men were sick with fever and so he decided to withdraw from an engagement. Sir Richard Grenville, in command of the *Revenge*, a ship of 500 tons, still had sick men ashore and felt compelled to remain until he had taken them on board. He was then cut off by the Spaniards from the main force. For fifteen hours he fought the Spanish fleet of over fifty ships. When most of his crew were dead and he was mortally wounded, he ordered the master-gunner to blow up the ship. The crew, however, surrendered and Sir Richard Grenville was taken aboard the Spanish flagship, where he died.

Sir Walter Raleigh in his *History of the World* gives the following account of the last action of the *Revenge*:

'All the powder of the *Revenge*, to the last barrel, was now spent, all their pikes were broken, forty of her best men slain, and the most part of the rest hurt. In the beginning of the fight she had but one hundred free from sickness, and fourscore and ten sick. A small troop to man such a ship, and a weak garrison to resist so mighty an army! By those hundred all was sustained, the volleys, boardings, and enterings of fifteen ships of war, besides those that beat her at large. On the contrary, the Spanish were always supplied with soldiers brought from every squadron; all manner of arms and powder at will. Unto ours there remained no comfort at all, no hope, no supply either of ships, men or weapons; the masts all beaten overboard, all her tackle cut asunder, her upper work altogether rased, nothing being left overhead either for flight or defence.

'Sir Richard now found himself in this distress, and unable any longer to make resistance. He had endured, in this fifteen hours' fight, the assault of fifteen several armadas, all by turns aboard him, and eight hundred shot of great artillery, besides many assaults and entries. He saw that he himself and the ship must needs be possessed by the enemy, who were now all cast in a ring about him; the *Revenge* not able to move one way or other, but as she was moved with the waves and billows of the sea. So he commanded the master gunner, whom he knew to be a most resolute man, to split and sink the ship, so that nothing might remain of glory or victory to the Spaniards. The master gunner readily condescended, and divers others; but the captain and the master were of another opinion.

'The master gunner, finding himself and Sir Richard thus prevented and mastered by the greater number, would have slain himself with a sword had he not been by force locked into his cabin. Then the Spanish general sent many boats aboard the *Revenge*.'

Read the poem to the class.

DRAMATIC PRESENTATION. Single speakers: Lord Howard, Sir Richard Grenville, a sailor, a narrator, a gunner.

Chorus divided into two groups: Group I, lighter voices; Group II, heavier voices.

The whole Chorus speaks the first two lines. Three voices from the Chorus speak the next line:

'Spanish ships of war at sea! we have sighted fifty-three!'

Narrator speaks the words introducing a single voice:

'Then sware Lord Thomas Howard:'

Then Lord Howard speaks boldly knowing that he is not foolhardy whatever others may judge him to be.

Narrator introduces the words of Sir Richard Grenville, spoken with a grave courtesy.

Group I of the Chorus speaks the whole of the third stanza.

Group II of the Chorus speaks the first part of the fourth stanza. The rest of the stanza is taken by the sailor, who is full of fear, and Sir Richard who replies with great good humour.

Group I speaks stanza V.

Group II speaks stanza VI.

Group II speaks first two lines of stanza VII and then whole Chorus speaks rest of stanza.

Both groups speak stanza VIII.

Group I. Three voices speak first two lines of stanza IX then joined by rest of group down to:

'with her battle-thunder and flame.'

Group II joins the rest in the next line and the whole Chorus build up to the climax in the last line:

'God of battles, was ever a battle like this in the world before?'

Narrator introduces stanza X. Sir Richard says, 'Fight on! fight on!'

Group I speaks the rest of the stanza up to the last line spoken by the Narrator and Sir Richard.

Group II speaks stanza XI down to the line:

'And the masts and the rigging were lying over the side.'

The Narrator speaks the next line and Sir Richard speaks proudly and boldly.

Narrator introduces stanza XII, the Gunner says 'Ay, ay,' the Narrator continues until the group of seamen, half of the group of heavier voices, speak their passionate protest.

The Narrator speaks the last line of the stanza.

Group I speaks the first part of stanza XIII.

Narrator speaks the line:

'But he rose upon their decks, and he cried:'

Sir Richard speaks his brave farewell.

Group I speaks the first part of stanza XIV down to the words 'down into the deep.'

Group II speaks the next four lines, and Group I joins at the line

'And or ever that evening ended...'

and the whole Chorus speaks the last six lines of the poem.

In this dramatic presentation try to bring out a sharp contrast between the characters of Lord Howard and Sir Richard Grenville, and show the fear of the sailor and the feelings of the group of seamen. The general feeling is one of danger, and there is power and dignity in the whole poem.

THE DESTRUCTION OF SENNACHERIB: LORD BYRON (p. 66)

AIM. To appreciate the dramatic qualities of the poem.

INTRODUCTION. Outline briefly the historical incident on which the poem is based. The episode is described in II Kings, chapters xviii and xix.

'Now in the fourteenth year of king Hezekiah did Sennacherib king of Assyria come up against all the fenced cities of Judah, and took them.... And the king of Assyria sent Tartan and Rabsaris and Rab-shakeh from Lachish to king Hezekiah with a great host against Jerusalem. And they went up and came to Jerusalem....And it came to pass that night, that the angel of the Lord went out, and smote in the camp of the Assyrians an hundred fourscore and five thousand: and when they arose early in the morning, behold, they were all dead corpses. So Sennacherib king of Assyria departed, and went and returned, and dwelt at Nineveh.'

Explain that Jerusalem was built on a hill, and the Assyrians pitched their tents in the valleys surrounding it.

Read the poem to the class. Read the poem again explaining the more difficult words.

Sennacherib: King of Assyria, 705–681 B.C.

Assyria: an ancient country situated in the valley of the river Tigris.

(It is now divided among Turkey, Iraq and Syria.)

Cohorts: armed troops.

Galilee: the Lake of Galilee, in Palestine.

Ashur: one of the chief towns of Assyria, situated on the river Tigris.

Baal: a god worshipped by the Phœnicians, Canaanites and others.

Gentile: anyone who was not a Jew.

DISCUSSION

How does the poet describe the size of the Assyrian host? The cohorts were so numerous that in the valley 'the sheen of their spears was like stars on the sea', and that host with their banners were 'like the leaves of the forest'.

How does he describe the strength and splendour of the Assyrians? They are dangerous, 'like the wolf on the fold' and splendid, 'gleaming in purple and gold'.

What contrast is made in the second stanza? The host is compared to the leaves of the forest in summer and then to the withered leaves of autumn. We are prepared for a disaster.

How are the terrible consequences of the plague caused by the visitation of the Angel of Death described? The poet gives vivid physical details of the effect of the plague upon the men and their horses. The eyes of the sleeping soldiers grew 'deadly and chill', their hearts heaved 'but once'; the horses lie dead with distended nostrils and the foam 'white on the turf'; the rider lies 'distorted and pale' a sign of his agony, 'the dew on his brow'.

Why are the idols in the temple of Baal broken?

DRAMATIC PRESENTATION. Divide the class into two groups, I and II. The combined groups speak verses 1, 3 and 6.

Group I speaks the first half of verses 2, 4 and 5.

Group II speaks the other half of verses 2, 4 and 5.

THE BATTLE OF THE BALTIC: THOMAS CAMPBELL (p. 71)

AIM. To appreciate the vigour of this poem which commemorates a great naval victory.

INTRODUCTION. Before reading the poem to the class, state briefly that the Battle of the Baltic was a naval battle fought off Copenhagen on 2 April 1801, in which a British fleet with Nelson as second-in-command annihilated the Danish navy.

Read the poem again.

DISCUSSION. The poet does not describe the battle in detail, but writes a rousing poem to commemorate the victory.

What is the theme of the first stanza? The might of the Danish fleet. Notice the use of short vigorous words, and the even distribution of strong stresses:

> 'When to báttle fiérce came fórth',
>
> 'By each gún the líghted bránd',
>
> 'And the Prínce of áll the lánd
>
> Léd them ón.'

This prepares us for the violent action which is to take place.

What is the theme of the second stanza? The suspense before the battle begins. Notice how skilfully the theme is presented. We are reminded of the might of the Danish fleet 'like leviathans afloat'. The sign of battle flies 'on the lofty British line'. Then we are told the exact hour, 'It was ten of April morn by the chime'—a vivid detail. The suspense is growing: the warships drift on their path (we can see them because of the word, 'drift') and we have 'the silence deep as death' and the boldest sailor holding his breath.

What part of the description in the third stanza do you find most effective? The short lines are admirably suited to express the eagerness of the English fleet to attack. Each phrase is strongly worded, and sound and image are admirably matched. Note the vigour of the lines:

> ...when each gún
>
> From its adamántine líps
>
> Spread a déath-sháde round the shíps,
>
> Like the húrricane eclípse
>
> Of the sún.

What contrasts are made in the fourth stanza? The violence of the

English attack is contrasted with the weakening of the Danish defence—the change from the arresting opening

Agaín! agaín! agaín!
And the hávoc did not slaćk,

to the slow heavy line—

Their shóts alóng the deép slówly boóm

is very marked, and the stanza ends with the ominous quiet of the lines:

'Or, in conflagration pale,
Light the gloom.'

What suggestions are made for celebrating this victory? Bonfires in the cities; drinking wine to the memory of those who fought.
What checks the feelings of joy? The thought of those who lie,

'Full many a fathom deep,
By thy wild and stormy steep,
Elsinore!'

Read the poem again.

THE BURIAL OF SIR JOHN MOORE AT CORUNNA: CHARLES WOLFE (p. 77)

AIM. To appreciate the sad dignity of this poem.

INTRODUCTION. Before reading the poem explain that Corunna is a port on the north coast of Spain to which Sir John Moore, the leader of the English troops in the Peninsular War, had been forced to retreat by the superior numbers of the French army. On 16 January 1809, Moore was killed in an engagement fought to cover the embarkation.

DISCUSSION

Why was Sir John Moore buried with such secrecy?
What phrases bring home to us most vividly the scene described?
Notice the deadening effect of the repeated negatives '*Not* a drum...', '*not* a funeral note', '*Not* a soldier...', '*No* useless coffin...', '*Not* in sheet *or* in shroud...', 'We spoke *not* a word of sorrow', '*not* a line', '*not* a stone'.

What restrained expressions show the soldiers' pride in their leader?
'Where our *hero* we buried', 'he lay like a *warrior*', 'we *bitterly*
thought of the morrow', 'we left him alone with his *glory*'.

What gives this poem such a restrained dignity? The sad subject is
presented in quiet measured tones. Many lines begin with a stressed
syllable:

> Not a drum was heard...
>
> Not a soldier discharged...
>
> Few and short were the prayers...
>
> Lightly they'll talk of the spirit

which imparts a grave, sad air to the poem. The stressed syllables
and long vowel sounds impel on us the way in which the poem must
be read:

> We thought, as we hollow'd his narrow bed
>
> And smoothed down his lonely pillow,
>
> That the foe and the stranger would tread o'er his head,
>
> And we far away on the billow!

What sounds are described in the poem?
The clock strikes 'the hour for retiring' and we hear

> 'the distant and random gun
> That the foe was sullenly firing.'

DRAMATIC PRESENTATION. Divide the class into two groups,
I and II.

Group I to take the first half of each verse.

Group II the rest of the verse.

Both groups combine to speak the last verse. The poem should be
spoken slowly and sadly.

THE CAVALIER'S ESCAPE: WALTER THORNBURY (p. 78)

AIM. To appreciate the vigorous movement of the poem.

INTRODUCTION. Read the poem to the class bringing out the
strongly marked rhythm. Read the poem again.

DISCUSSION

What is the theme of the poem? The desperate ride of a cavalier who is pursued by his enemies for five miles to Salisbury town.

What words are used to give the sound of the hoofs of galloping horses? 'Trample! trample!', 'Trap! trap!', 'Pad! pad! pad!', 'Thud! thud!', 'Rap! rap!' Notice how these different sounds describe the hoofs on stones and roads, grassland, 'the level sward', and sand.

What other examples are there where the sound of the word suits the sense?

'They *splashed* through miry rut and pool—
   Splintered through fence and rail;
But chestnut Kate *switched* over the gate—
   I saw them *droop* and tail.'

'The roan flew on at a *staggering* pace.'

How many horses are mentioned in the poem? Three. The cavalier's chestnut mare, the roan (brown and white in colour) and the grey.

What words and phrases describe the superiority of the cavalier's chestnut mare?

'My chestnut broke away.'
'But my chestnut mare was of blood so rare,
   That she showed them all the way.'
'But chestnut Kate switched over the gate.'

The other horses splash through pools, splinter through fence and rail, but Kate jumps cleanly over.

'But blood is better than bone.'
'For I knew it was all my own.'

Why are the hoofs said to be 'echoing' in stanza IV? Because they are galloping 'past the walls of mossy stone' which would give back the sound.

Why does the cavalier say 'I saw their wolf's eyes burn'? Because they pursue him like a pack of wolves, and they are relentless and full of hate.

Why does he have to turn and fight? Some of his pursuers had

headed him off. He strikes one down, slices the crown of another
and then rides through the rest

'Fast, fast, to Salisbury town.'

What was the 'burning match'? The burning tow used to fire
a match-lock musket.

What is meant by 'a shaking of flag and hand'? The pursuers, as
a last act of defiance, shake the flag they have been carrying and
clench their fists at the gate of Salisbury, a Royalist stronghold.

What is the meaning of the word 'canting'? A term of abuse
meaning insincerely pious, full of smug hypocrisy.

DRAMATIC PRESENTATION. This poem lends itself to vigorous
choral reading. Divide the class into two groups, I and II.

STANZA I: Group I, first line.
              Group II, second line.
              Full chorus, rest of the stanza.

STANZA II: Group I, first line.
              Group II, second line.
              Full chorus, rest of the stanza.

STANZA III: Group I, first line.
              Group II, second line.
              Full chorus, rest of the stanza.

STANZA IV: Group I, first two lines.
              Group II, next two lines.
              Full chorus, rest of the stanza.

STANZA V: Group I, first line.
              Group II, second line.
              Full chorus, rest of the stanza.

STANZA VI: Group I, first two lines.
              Group II, next two lines.
              Full chorus, rest of the stanza.

STANZA VII: Group I, first line.
              Group II, second line.
              Group I, third line.
              Group II, fourth line.
              Full chorus, last two lines.

HOW THEY BROUGHT THE GOOD NEWS FROM GHENT TO AIX:
ROBERT BROWNING (p. 80)

AIM. To appreciate the galloping rhythm and vigorous story-telling of this poem.

INTRODUCTION. Before reading the poem to the class, explain certain words such as postern, girths, pique, cheek-strap, croup; then read the poem bringing out the galloping rhythm.

DISCUSSION. In reading the poem one may not grasp immediately the situation.

How many riders are there and how are they mounted? The Narrator is riding Roland, Joris is riding the roan, Dirck is riding Roos.

How many reach Aix, what happens to the others? The Narrator on Roland is the only one to reach Aix; Dirck's mare fails by Hasselt

'down on her haunches she shuddered and sank'.

Joris's roan rolls 'neck and croup over' 'dead as a stone' when Aix is in sight.

How is the progress of their exciting ride indicated? We are told both the time and the place throughout the ride. They leave Ghent as 'the lights sank to rest' and they gallop 'into the midnight'. They approach Lokeren and 'twilight dawned clear'. At Boom 'a great yellow star' appears. At Düffeld it is morning. They hear the half-chime from the church-steeple at Mecheln. At Aershot the sun rises. It is now day as they gallop through Hasselt. Here Dirck drops out. Past Looz and Tongres 'the broad sun above laughed a pitiless laugh'. They see the white dome-spire near Dalhem, and here Joris falls out of the race. The Narrator, on Roland, gallops into Aix. This resounding roll of the names of towns and the description of the change from midnight through dawn to day gives the excitement of a real event to the poem.

How are we told of the urgency of the ride? The three riders are urged on by the cry 'Good speed!' The word 'Speed!' echoes in their ears. They say 'not a word to each other'. They keep the great pace grimly riding 'never changing place'. Then the Narrator makes adjustments to girths, stirrups, pique, cheek-strap, bit, while Roland gallops as steadily as before.

What indications are there of the quality of Roland? Roland is so well trained that he can gallop without changing pace while his harness is adjusted. His power is described 'stout galloper', 'resolute shoulders'; his intelligence in his understanding of his master 'just one sharp ear bent back for my voice', 'one eye's black intelligence'; his carriage and endurance are described in stanza VIII.

> 'With his nostrils like pits full of blood to the brim,
> And with circles of red for his eye-sockets' rim.'

He is a 'horse without peer'.

Why does the Narrator throw off his clothing? He realizes that his horse is almost spent. He throws off his clothing to lighten the load. He does everything he can think of to encourage Roland to keep on, urging him on by making any noise 'bad or good'.

DRAMATIC PRESENTATION. The rhythm of the verse suggests admirably the sound of galloping horses:

> I sprang to the stirrup, and Joris, and he;
> I galloped, Dirck galloped, we galloped all three;
> 'Good speed!' cried the watch, as the gate-bolts undrew;
> 'Speed!' echoed the wall to us galloping through.

Divide the class into two groups, I and II, and have single voices for Joris and the watch.

Each group to speak alternate stanzas, and the full chorus to speak the last stanza.

THE POET AND THE MODERN WORLD

THE SECRET OF THE MACHINES: RUDYARD KIPLING (p. 107)

AIM. To appreciate the poet's attitude to the world of machines.

INTRODUCTION. Read the poem to the class bringing out the strong staccato rhythm suggesting the regular throbbing of a machine.

DISCUSSION

What is the poet describing in the first stanza? The making of modern machinery adapted to many different purposes. Get the class to name some of these, indicated in the four-line stanza

'We can pull and haul and push and lift and drive.'

What is the theme of the second eight-line stanza? The telephone and the Atlantic liner. The description of the liner is continued into the four-line stanza. Note the contrast 'the captain turns the lever' and the 'monstrous nine-decked city goes to sea'.

What activities are described in the third eight-line stanza? Notice how much the poet compresses into this stanza and the next. *What phrases are particularly effective?*

What is the Law by which the machines live? They have no feelings, can do only that for which they were designed, and mis-handled they are dangerous.

Is it true to say that machines 'are greater than the Peoples or the Kings'? They are not greater because they are conceived and made by the people. But there is some truth in the remark that man may become the slave of the machine.

Give examples where the touch of machines has altered 'created things'.

CHORAL READING. Divide the class into four groups, I, II, III and IV. Each group should read one eight-line stanza.

Groups I and II to read the four-line stanza beginning: 'We can pull and haul...' and the one beginning:

'The boat-express is waiting....'

Groups III and IV to read the four-line stanza beginning:

'It is easy! Give us dynamite....'

The full chorus to read the last four lines of the poem:

'*Though our smoke may hide the Heavens from your eyes....*'

THE PIGEON: RICHARD CHURCH (p. 108)

AIM. To appreciate how poetry is made out of the common objects of the modern industrial world.

INTRODUCTION. Read the poem and ask for general comments on first impressions. Read the poem again.

DISCUSSION

What is the theme of the poem?

What are the feelings of the poet about the scene he describes? Feelings of distaste. This is shown by the words and phrases he uses in the description:

'*Spewing* out concrete.'

'Stand the *serpent-warders,*
Sweating and *straining,*
Thrusting those *cruel* mouths to their prey.'

'...the steel tongues *hiss*
As they *stab.*'

'The *clatter* that *shatters* the brain.'

What attracts the attention of the crowd?

'...the flat, wet levels
Of newlaid cement.'

'And a pigeon from a plane-tree
Flutters down to bathe its wings in that mirage of water.'

What lines in the previous stanza prepare us for the mistake the pigeon makes? The wet levels of newlaid cement are described as: 'those curdled lakes' that 'glisten under the sky'.

What words describe the reactions of the pigeon? It is deceived by the 'mirage of water', angry at the deception, and bewildered by the din from the cement-mixer.

What contrast is presented in this poem? The contrast between the cement-mixer spewing out concrete and the pigeon 'from a plane-tree' which are brought together for a moment, and such is the poet's art that we are left with the image, 'the seal' of the pigeon's 'coral foot' in the concrete, something of beauty in the ugliness of the scene.

PRELUDE: T. S. ELIOT (p. III)

AIM. To consider whether the imagery is appropriate to the subject and mood of the poem.

INTRODUCTION. Read the poem to the class and ask for general comments on first impressions. Read the poem again.

DISCUSSION. All poets are not concerned with the portrayal of beauty, and we should not look for 'beautiful' imagery in all the verse we read. Some poets protest against the ugliness of the modern world in verse that reflects that ugliness. Remember you must judge the poet in accordance with what he is trying to do. He may do anything he pleases, provided he can do it. You must be prepared to revise your presuppositions as to what poetry should be.

This poem is an impressionistic description of a sordid scene. The imagery is deliberately unromantic.

What line may be said to sum up the theme of the poem?

'The burnt-out ends of smoky days.'

What words and phrases help to create the mood of despondency?

'Burnt-out ends of smoky days.'
'Gusty shower.'
'Grimy scraps.'
'Newspapers from vacant lots.'
'Broken blinds.'
'A lonely cab-horse steams and stamps.'

Is the poet successful in achieving his purpose?
Read the poem again.

TO IRON-FOUNDERS AND OTHERS: GORDON BOTTOMLEY (p. 113)

AIM. To share imaginatively the poet's feeling of anger at the encroachments on the countryside by the iron-founders.

INTRODUCTION. Read the poem and ask for general comments on first impressions.

DISCUSSION

What is the theme of the poem? That to destroy grass and the 'green life' on which man lives, by digging iron ore from the earth to make 'machines for making more machines', can only lead to disaster. Nature must ultimately triumph and man will learn again to fashion ploughs 'to wake grass in every field'.

How does the poet reveal his anger? He uses powerful expressions:

'You *poison* England at her roots.'

'Where your *unnatural* vapours creep.'

'Your worship is your furnaces,
    Which, *like old idols, lost obscenes,*
Have molten bowels.'

'O, you are *busied in the night,*
    Preparing destinies *of rust.*'

Do you consider his anger is justified?

How does he express the struggle which Nature makes against the encroachments of industry? Though grass has gone, other plants continue to grow in ruins and shards. Nature is still there in attendance until this 'dream is done'.

Where does he say that Nature will finally triumph? In the verse:

'The generations of the worm
    Know not your loads piled on their soil;
Their knotted ganglions shall wax firm
    Till your strong flagstones heave and toil.'

The thought expressed here is developed in the next two verses to reach the final affirmation that man will again make simple implements—

'Ploughs to wake grass in every field,
    Chisels men's hands to magnify.'

Read the poem again.

PART IV

THE MUSIC OF POETRY

HYMN TO DIANA: BEN JONSON (p. 126)

AIM. To appreciate the stately, dignified movement of this lyrical poem.

INTRODUCTION. Read the poem to the class slowly, allowing the lovely sound of the words to have their full effect. Read again for the smooth sweeping beauty of the verbal music.

DISCUSSION

What is the subject of the poem? The poem is a hymn in adoration of Diana (or Cynthia) the goddess of the moon. She was also the goddess of the chase, depicted with bow and quiver of arrows. Diana was worshipped as the goddess of chastity.

The poem is constructed on a complicated pattern and deserves close analysis. The tone of the poem, that is the 'manner of reading compelled upon one' is dignified, stately, serene. This is achieved by the careful choice of words: 'Queen', 'chaste', 'fair', 'silver', 'manner', 'goddess', 'bright'; and on the arrangement of the words for their sound, stress and movement.

> Queen and huntress, ‖ chaste and fair, ‖
> Now the sun is laid to sleep, ‖
> Seated in thy silver chair, ‖
> State in wonted manner keep: ‖
> Hesperus entreats thy light, ‖
> Goddess ‖ excellently bright.

The use of the trochaic foot (′ ˘) at the beginning of each line instead of the more usual iambic foot (˘ ′) gives the slow emphasis and stately movement which is maintained throughout the poem by a masterly use of vowel sounds, alliteration, and the caesura.

CHORAL READING. Divide the class into four groups, I, II, III and IV.

STANZA I

Group I should speak the first line.
Group II should speak the second line.
Group I should speak the third and fourth lines.
Both groups join to speak the last two lines.

STANZA II

Group III should speak the first two lines.
Group IV should speak the next two lines.
Both groups join to speak the last two lines.

STANZA III

Group I should speak the first line.
Group II should speak the second line.
Group III should speak the third and fourth lines.
Group IV should speak the last two lines.

SONG FOR ST CECILIA'S DAY: JOHN DRYDEN (p. 128)

AIM. To appreciate the richness of sound and in choral speaking to practise the use of increasing and reducing of voices.

INTRODUCTION. This poem demands some explanation before it is read to the class.

It is a song in honour of music of which Cecilia was patron saint. She was a Christian martyr who died in Rome in A.D. 230, was supposed to have played an organ and was regarded as the patroness of church music.

The first verse refers to the ancient theory of the creation of the universe according to which all matter consisted of a chaos of atoms of four types, cold, hot, moist and dry. These 'jarring atoms' were reduced to order by the harmonizing influence of music. The diapason was the series of harmonious sounds concluding in the creation of man.

Jubal, according to the Book of Genesis (chapter iv, *vv.* 19–21), was 'the father of all such as handle the harp and organ'. The 'corded shell' is a hollow shell with strings stretched across it.

Orpheus, according to Greek mythology, played the lyre so sweetly that savage animals and even inanimate objects followed him. The music of the spheres mentioned in the Grand Chorus is explained as the theory of a Greek philosopher, Pythagoras, who proclaimed that the planets made harmonious sounds as they moved through space.

The last line of the poem says that just as music by its harmony helped in the ordering of the universe so when 'the last and dreadful hour' comes music will help in the final dissolution.

CHORAL SPEAKING. For this arrangement I am indebted to Miss Mona Swann's *Many Voices*, Part I.

Divide the class into four groups:

Group I. Strongest voices to take the description of the trumpets and drums.
Group II. The lightest of all to take the flute.
Group III. The second strongest to take the harp and organ.
Group IV. Medium voices to take the violins.

The whole class speaks the first two lines which introduce the theme.

Groups II and III speak lines 3 to 10, the rest of the stanza is spoken by Groups I and IV, joined in the last two lines by Groups II and III which brings in all voices at line 14.

The whole class speaks the first line of the next stanza, the rest of the stanza is spoken by Group III.

Group I speaks the description of trumpet and drum.
Group II speaks that of the flute.
Group IV speaks that of the violins.

The whole class again comes in on the first line of the stanza beginning:
'But O! what art can teach'

and speaks the whole of this stanza.

Group III speaks the stanza beginning:

> 'Orpheus could lead the savage race.'

Group III speaks the first two lines of the Grand Chorus, and is joined at the third line by Group II; at line 5 Group IV is added and three lines later Group I joins in; the whole class is thus speaking the last two lines.

Particular attention should be paid to phrasing, and the aim of the class should be to give both power and dignity to the poem.

THE REAPER: WILLIAM WORDSWORTH (p. 131)

AIM. To appreciate the imagery and the lyrical beauty of this poem.

INTRODUCTION. Read the poem to the class. Then give briefly the following information.

In September 1803, Wordsworth and his sister Dorothy were walking in Scotland near Loch Katrine and Ben Lomond. Dorothy tells in her *Journal* how they had been passing 'through coppices or open fields, and passing farm-houses though always with an inter-mixture of uncultivated ground. It was harvest time and the fields were quietly (might I be allowed to say pensively?) enlivened by small companies of reapers. It is not uncommon in the more lonely parts of the Highlands to see a *single* person so employed.'

Read the poem again. Read the last stanza of Wordsworth's *The Daffodils*. Point out the similarity between the experience expressed in these lines:

> 'They flash upon that inward eye
> Which is the bliss of solitude;
> And then my heart with pleasure fills,
> And dances with the daffodils'

and the last two lines of *The Reaper*.

DISCUSSION

What is the theme of the poem? A highland reaper, working by herself, sings a melancholy song which holds the attention of the poet. He describes its effect upon him, and wonders what the subject of her song may be.

How does the poet describe the effect of the girl's singing upon him?
In the second stanza, in glowing romantic language, he says that
no nightingale 'did ever chaunt more welcome notes', and that

> 'A voice so thrilling ne'er was heard
> In spring-time from the cuckoo-bird.'

By referring to the song of the nightingale and the cuckoo he gives
the *thrilling* quality of the reaper's song.

Explain carefully the significance of the last two lines:

> 'The music in my heart I bore,
> Long after it was heard no more.'

CHORAL SPEAKING. Divide the class into four groups, two with
light and two with heavier voices.

The heavier voices speak the first and the last stanzas.

The lighter voices speak the second and third stanzas.

BLOW, BUGLE, BLOW: LORD TENNYSON (p. 132)

AIM. To appreciate the music and the imaginative power of the
poem.

INTRODUCTION. Read the poem through once, bringing out the
sounds so that one can hear the bugle and its fading echoes repeated
again and again. Read the poem a second time for the imagery.

CHORAL READING. This song should be spoken in unison, and it
is not easy to say it well. Work out the pattern of sound in the first
stanza with great care.

> The splendour falls on castle walls
> And snowy summits old in story:
> The long light shakes across the lakes,
> And the wild cataract leaps in glory.
> Blow, bugle, blow, set the wild echoes flying,
> Blow, bugle; answer, echoes, dying, dying, dying.

Notice the third line where we have five stressed syllables and the
liquid 'l' sound suggests the 'level lakes'. The next line is in sharp

contrast, with its sudden change in rhythm and the word cataract (with its dactyllic stress) giving the violence of leaping water.

The last two lines must be said quietly and with a gradual decrease in sound.

The second stanza must be 'thin and clear' as the words themselves imply. The lines:

> 'O sweet and far from cliff and scar
> The horns of Elfland faintly blowing!'

must be clearly enunciated, paying particular attention to the 'f' sounds.

The third stanza gives opportunities for contrast between the thin sounds in the first two lines:

> '...they die in yon rich sky
> They faint on hill or field or river'

and the full vowel sounds in the third and fourth lines.

> 'Our echoes roll from soul to soul,
> And grow for ever and for ever.'

THE LOTOS-EATERS: LORD TENNYSON (p. 133)

AIM. To appreciate the music of the lines and to consider the craftsmanship of the poet.

INTRODUCTION. Outline briefly the story of Ulysses and mention some of his adventures. Tell the class that he came to the island of the lotos-eaters who fed strangers on the fruit of the lotos. This produced complete forgetfulness of home, family and past life. What sort of island would the class imagine this to be? What sort of climate, vegetation would it have? What sort of people would the lotos-eaters themselves be? Such questions should stimulate the interest and the imagination of the class.

Read the poem.

DISCUSSION

How far does the description in the poem resemble what the class had already imagined?

What passages in the poem are particularly effective? Why?

What passages are remarkable for their sound?

Select a passage for more detailed appreciation.

The Lotos blooms below the barren peak:
The Lotos blows by every winding creek:
All day the wind breathes low with mellower tone:
Through every hollow cave and alley lone
Round and round the spicy downs the yellow Lotos-dust is blown.
We have had enough of action, and of motion we,
Rolled to starboard, rolled to larboard, when the surge was seething
   free,
Where the wallowing monster spouted his foam-fountains in the
   sea.

Here we have sound following effortlessly the sense, giving the
feeling of languorous ease where the lotos blooms. Long vowel
sounds give the mellow flute-like note, and the replication of consonant sounds weaves a subtle tapestry of song. Consider the use
of the letters 'l', 'b', and 'm' in the first three lines, and the sound
of the words in the last line where the use of 's', 't' and 'f' creates
a living picture of the sea-spouting whale.

CHORAL SPEAKING. Divide the class into four groups, one with
the heaviest voices Group I, one with the lightest voices Group II,
two groups, III and IV, with medium voices.

   Group II speaks the first section of the poem down to '...poppy
hangs in sleep'. Group I speaks the next section, down to 'Why
should we only toil, the roof and crown of things?' Group III
speaks the section beginning 'Lo! in the middle of the wood', down
to '...in the fruitful soil'. Group IV speaks the next section
'Hateful is the dark-blue sky...', down to 'dark death, or dreamful
ease'. Group II speaks the following section, down to '...shut in an
urn of brass!' Group I speaks the next section, down to '...gazing
on the pilot-stars'. Group III speaks the following section, down to
'...stretched out beneath the pine'. Group II speaks the next
section and is joined by Group I at the line 'We have had enough

of action....' Groups III and IV join the other two groups at the line beginning 'For they lie beside their nectar...' and the whole class speaks in unison to the end of the poem.

L'ALLEGRO: JOHN MILTON (p. 137)

AIM. To appreciate the infinite variety of the music of the poem and the quality of the imagery.

INTRODUCTION. Read the poem to the class bringing out the smooth, effortless flow of the verse.

DISCUSSION. The delicate grace of this poem can be readily seen: it has a freshness and charm which Milton never recaptured. The poet uses many devices to give the verse this delicate movement. The poem is written in octosyllabic rhyming couplets with a frequent use of the seven instead of the normal eight syllable line. The normal line is iambic:

> To hear the lark begin his flight.

Where a seven syllable line is used, the first, unaccentuated syllable is omitted:

> Haste thee, Nymph, and bring with thee
> Jest, and youthful Jollity,
> Quips and Cranks and wanton Wiles,
> Nods and Becks and wreathèd Smiles.

This variation of trochaic and iambic feet gives not only lightness of touch but speed of movement, the easy tripping metre. The placing of the caesura, or pause, at the end or inside the line is skilfully varied to avoid all possibility of monotony:

> Come, ‖ and trip it, ‖ as you go, ‖
> On the light fantastic toe; ‖
> And in thy right hand lead with thee ‖
> The mountain nymph, ‖ sweet Liberty; ‖
> And, ‖ if I give thee honour due, ‖
> Mirth, ‖ admit me of thy crew, ‖
> To live with her, ‖ and live with thee, ‖
> In unreprovèd pleasures free. ‖

Comment on the poet's use of personification which is a feature of the poem.

> 'Sport that wrinkled Care derides,
> And Laughter holding both his sides.'

Here Sport, Care and Laughter, instead of being abstractions become living persons: we see 'wrinkled' Care; and Laughter 'holding both his sides' is vividly realized.

The class should consider carefully the aptness of the imagery and select what they think are the best examples. Notice the accuracy of the poet's observation:

> 'Till the *dappled* dawn doth rise.'

> 'While the Cock with *lively din*,
> Scatters the rear of *darkness thin*;
> And to the stack, or the barn-door,
> *Stoutly struts* his dames before.'

Not only are the sights and sounds of the English countryside accurately and lovingly described, but in the expression the sound suits exactly the sense and gives that satisfaction that comes from the finest poetry.

SCENES OF THE MACHINE AGE

MORNING EXPRESS: SIEGFRIED SASSOON (p. 151)

AIM. To appreciate the pictorial and sound effects in this descriptive poem.

INTRODUCTION. Read the poem and ask for general comments on first impressions. Read the poem again bringing out the full effect of those words used to imitate the sounds they describe.

DISCUSSION. This poem not only describes the scene in telling detail, but also by carefully chosen words imitates the sounds described.

What expressions are particularly effective in describing the scene?

'Offering themselves to morn's long slanting arrows.'
'...clouds of sun-blown vapour.'
'Glide the processional windows on their way.'
'...drifting banners tell
Their progress to the counties.'

What expressions are particularly effective in describing the sounds?

'...others *rumble* the milk in gleaming cans.'
'...with *clang* and *clack*,
Touches and tests, and listens to the wheels.'
'the monster *grunts*: "*Enough!*"
Tightening his load of links with pant and puff.'

In this expression we hear the sound of the steam in 'grunts: "Enough!"', and in the next line the clatter of couplings as they take the strain.

Explain the meaning of:

'drifting banners tell
Their progress to the counties.'

Read the poem again.

THE BRIDGE: JOHN REDWOOD ANDERSON (p. 151)

AIM. To appreciate the vigour of the poem, and the adaptation of poetic imagery to a new industrial age.

INTRODUCTION. Read the poem to the class bringing out the vigour of expression. Read the poem again.

DISCUSSION

What is the keynote of this poem?
The poet gives a flying movement from the first line:

> 'Here, with one *leap*,
> The bridge that *spans* the cutting....'

The railway lines *sweep*

> 'Into the solitary plains.'

The sky is full of movement too:

> 'The whole east *rushes down* them with its light.'

There is no pause in this movement, which rises to its climax when the train comes

> 'Out of the silence grows
> An iron thunder—grows, and roars, and sweeps,
> Menacing!'

We have a crescendo of sound—

> 'The plain
> Suddenly leaps,
> Startled, from its repose...',

then

> 'Louder the throb and roar of wheels,
> The shout of speed, the shriek of steam'

while

> '...the ground
> Shudders and the bridge reels—'

and the train is flashing past

> 'A rage of smoke, a laugh of fire,
> A lighted anguish of desire...'

123

as the train roars past—

> 'The plain,
> Shaken, exultant, unconfined,
> Rises, flows on, and follows, and sweeps by,
> Shrieking, to lose itself in distance and the sky.'

There is no variation in this poem, from beginning to end it rattles past with something of the speed it describes.

Where do you imagine the poet-observer to be standing? On the bridge. From here he describes the scene—the bridge itself, the cutting, the main road, the railway track. Then he describes the railway lines stretching out into 'the solitary plains asleep'. Suddenly he sees the signal change from red to green. He hears the train, sees it approaching, feels it thundering past; with the tumultuous moment he mentions the plain which seems to follow the flying movement of the train.

Why does the poet say the railway lines are 'like arms of mute appeal'? What are they appealing for? The train to come; it is for the train that they exist and the poet imagines them crying, calling, appealing for the train to come.

How is the train personified? The train is described as a rage of smoke, a laugh of fire, a lighted anguish of desire; rage, laughter, anguish and desire are all human attributes. The words

> 'A dream
> Of gold and iron'

suggest human personality.

How is the plain personified? The words 'shaken', 'exultant', 'unconfined' suggest, again, human qualities. The plain is said to rise, sweep on and follow the disappearing train. The observer standing on the bridge sees the train disappear in a swirl of smoke and steam, and it is as though it has gathered up part of the country-side as it rushes through the cutting and under the bridge. Thus the plain appears to be following

> 'Shrieking, to lose itself in distance and the sky.'

Read the poem again.

THE EXPRESS: STEPHEN SPENDER (p. 153)

AIM. To appreciate the sound and imagery of this poem in the modern idiom.

INTRODUCTION. In order to show how the new things of a new world have been accepted, absorbed and turned into poetry, read first of all the following passage from Tennyson's *Princess*:

> 'round the lake
> A little clock-work steamer paddling plied
> And shook the lilies: perch'd about the knolls
> A dozen angry models jetted steam:
> A petty railway ran: a fire-balloon
> Rose gem-like up before the dusky groves
> And dropt a fairy parachute and past:
> And there through twenty posts of telegraph
> They flash'd a saucy message to and fro
> Between the mimic stations; so that sport
> Went hand in hand with science.'

Then read the poem, asking the class to notice the differences in tone and expression. Read the poem again bringing out the rhythmic movement suggesting an express train going at full speed:

> ...at lást with a jázzy mádness—
> The sóng of her whístle scréaming at cúrves,
> Of deáfening túnnels, brákes, innúmerable bólts.
> And álways líght, aérial, underneath
> Góes the eláte métre of her whéels.

DISCUSSION

What lines and phrases suggest the familiar sounds of an express train?

Point out how in a line like the first one—

'After the first powerful plain manifesto'

we have the slow compressed strength of the engine in the words 'powerful plain' and the hiss of steam in the word 'manifesto'. There are, of course, many lines suggesting the sounds of an express

STORIES OF PURE IMAGINATION

THE DIRGE OF LOVELY ROSABELLE:
SIR WALTER SCOTT (p. 161)

AIM. To appreciate the eeriness of the poem, and the highly imaginative narrative skill of the poet.

INTRODUCTION. It is well to give a brief outline of the substance of the poem.

Rosabelle, a daughter of the St Clairs, had left her home, Roslin Castle, situated on the south side of the Firth of Forth, to visit friends at Ravensheuch, a castle on a steep crag on the other side of the Firth. Feeling that her mother was lonely she decided to return home in spite of the warnings of the boatman that a storm was brewing. The fishermen said that they had heard the screams of the Water-Sprite which foretold a shipwreck. Rosabelle ignored these warnings, attempted to cross the river; a storm blew up, and she was drowned. According to legend whenever one of the family of St Clair was close to death 'a spectral light shone on the rock of Roslin Castle and at the Chapel'. This light was seen during the night when Rosabelle was drowned. By it her parents knew of her death and the prophecies of disaster were fulfilled.

It must be clearly stated that this summary cannot stand in the place of the poem, which is an imaginative experience. We must consider the way in which the poet has presented this story to give it imaginative force.

Read the poem. Read the poem a second time giving the following brief explanations.

inch: an island.
Water-Sprite: a spirit, whose screams foretold disaster.
Seer: a man with the power to see into the future.

The ring they ride: an exercise where a man on horseback charged past a suspended ring and tried to carry it off on the point of his spear.

Hawthornden: a narrow glen running north from Roslin Castle.

chapel proud: the chapel stands beside Roslin Castle and contains a famous carved pillar.

panoply: complete armour.

sacristy: the room where the sacred vessels, books, and vestments were kept.

pale: a boundary.

pinnet: a pinnacle.

DISCUSSION

How does the poem differ in its presentation of the story from the summary? The poem is carefully arranged so that it creates suspense, works up to a climax and moves us by the dramatic fulfilment of the prophecy. Note how the poet has changed the order of events. He begins in the middle of the narrative without any explanation, in the manner of the old ballads. We are told of the dreadful warning, of the vision of the Seer. Suspense, a sense of foreboding, are created. The usual directions to indicate the speaker are omitted. Rosabelle answers the boatman:

> ''Tis not because Lord Lindesay's heir
> To-night at Roslin leads the ball,
> But that my ladye-mother there
> Sits lonely in her castle-hall.'

We have the utmost economy and directness in the telling.

We know Rosabelle has set out across the Firth. Immediately, the spectral light blazes

> 'O'er Roslin all that dreary night'

the words of the legend are fulfilled. In five vivid stanzas the blazing lights are described. This supernatural and terrible event is not explained, we are left with the mystery. At the end of the poem we are told briefly that Rosabelle has been drowned

> 'But the sea holds lovely Rosabelle!'

and in muted sounds

> 'the sea-caves rung, and the wild winds sung,
> The dirge of lovely Rosabelle.'

Read the poem again to bring out the points mentioned in the discussion.

LA BELLE DAME SANS MERCI: JOHN KEATS (p. 189)

AIM. To appreciate the dream-world atmosphere and the haunting power of this short poem.

INTRODUCTION. Read the poem to the class. Read the poem again asking the class to consider whether it is a dream, a story of enchantment, or does the Narrator dream of the knight-at-arms?

DISCUSSION. The poet has been thinking of the medieval world of chivalry, and he writes in the form and style of the old ballads miraculously catching the very sense of mystery and romance.

What are we told? A knight-at-arms, questioned by a stranger, tells how he met a lady in the meads, a faery's child. He fell under her enchantment, set her on his 'pacing steed'

> 'And nothing else saw all day long.'

She took him to her elfin grot and there lulled him to sleep. Is this a real happening? In his sleep he dreams

> 'On the cold hill's side'

of pale kings and princes, pale warriors: are these all the victims of the faery lady? They warn him

> '...La belle Dame sans Merci
> Hath thee in thrall!'

Is this his dream within a dream? He wakes to find himself on the 'cold hill's side'. This is reality. But the dream, or the mysterious experience he has had leaves him sad and bewildered. His mood is wonderfully expressed in the closing lines of the poem

> 'Alone and palely loitering,
> Though the sedge is wither'd from the lake,
> And no birds sing.'

By the magic of words, Keats has created a world of the imagination. We enter it when we read the poem and it fills our minds with imagery and sound.

Notice the wonderful economy of expression and the music of each verse, with the haunting sound of the last line of each verse.

KUBLA KHAN: SAMUEL TAYLOR COLERIDGE (p. 195)

AIM. To appreciate the beauty of the poetic world this poem creates.

INTRODUCTION. Without laying too much stress upon it, one might outline briefly the circumstances of the composition of this poem.

Coleridge was staying in a Devonshire farm-house. He had taken some tincture of opium to deaden the pain of neuralgia from which he suffered, and was drowsily reading an account of China in *Purchas his Pilgrimes*. The last words he read before he fell asleep were these:

'In Xamdiu did Cublai Can build a stately Palace, encompassing sixteene miles of plaine ground with a wall, wherein are fertile Meddowes, pleasant springs, delightfull Streames, and all sorts of beasts of chase and game, and in the middest thereof a sumptuous house of pleasure.'

He slept for some hours and he dreamed. The images of the dream and words and phrases describing those images formed together in his mind so that when he awoke he had a complete poem of about 200 lines in his head. He began to write it down in a state of excitement. When he had written about fifty lines he was interrupted by a man knocking on the door who had come from Porlock. This visitor detained Coleridge for nearly an hour. When he left, Coleridge found that the rest of the poem had vanished from his mind except for one or two words and phrases.

Read the poem bringing out the lovely sound of the words.

DISCUSSION. The imagery and word music combine to create a romantic dream world. The opening lines have a lulling, hypnotic effect with their smooth rhythm (the repetition of stress), their alliteration (the repetition of consonants) and their rhyme (the repetition of similar sounds).

> In Xanadu did Kubla Khan
> A stately pleasure-dome decree:
> Where Alph, the sacred river, ran
> Through caverns measureless to man
> Down to a sunless sea.

Coleridge recalls the most romantic associations in the lines:

> 'A savage place! as holy and enchanted
> As e'er beneath a waning moon was haunted
> By woman wailing for her demon-lover!'

Notice how in the line:

> 'Five miles meandering with a mazy motion'

the use of the long vowel sounds and the use of the letter 'm' make the line itself move slowly, meandering like the scene it describes.

Throughout the poem Coleridge refers to the romantically distant in time and place to enrich the dream world he creates using romantic proper names—Xanadu, Kubla Khan, Alph the sacred river, the Abyssinian maid, Mount Abora.

The last section of the poem may need a little explanation.

Coleridge says that if he could revive within himself the 'symphony and song' of the Abyssinian maid, that is, develop the real power of poetry (as *she* had the real power of song) then he would re-create in words the perfect beauty of Kubla Khan's palace, 'that dome in air', and people would declare him to be divinely inspired, feeding on honey-dew and the milk of Paradise beyond the limitations of mortal men.

THE LISTENERS: WALTER DE LA MARE (p. 218)

AIM. To appreciate the mysteriousness of the poem.

INTRODUCTION. Read the poem to the class. Ask for their general comments on first impressions. Read the poem through again.

DISCUSSION

What contrast is presented in the poem? The contrast between the 'host of phantom listeners' inside the still house and the Traveller and his horse from the outside world.

How is the 'lone house' made mysterious? By the sense of silent isolation. It is night-time. The Traveller knocks on the 'moonlit door'. The house is in the middle of a forest removed from 'the world of men'. A host of phantom listeners live in the house. They listen in 'the quiet of the moonlight'. Faint moonbeams 'fall on the dark stair'. The emptiness of the house is emphasized.

> 'And a bird flew up out of the turret.'

> 'No head from the leaf-fringed sill
> Lean'd over and look'd into his grey eyes.'

There is the quiet of the moonlight; the empty hall. No one answered.

> '. . . the silence surged softly backward,
> When the plunging hoofs were gone.'

What are we told about the Traveller? He knocks on the door, saying, 'Is there anybody there?' His horse champed the grasses; it moves cropping the dark turf apparently undisturbed by his master's uneasiness. The Traveller knocks on the door again, more loudly, and says,

> 'Tell them I came, and no one answer'd,
> That I kept my word.'

He is the 'one man left awake'. He puts his foot in the stirrup, mounts his horse; there is the sound of iron hoofs on stone and he rides away.

How does the poet develop the mysteriousness of the story? The subject is presented by carefully chosen details in the opening lines. We have the Traveller knocking on the moonlit door, his horse feeds on the grass, a bird flies up out of the turret. The question, 'Is there anybody there?' is unanswered. It is repeated. Still there is no answer. The Traveller is perplexed. Then we are told of a host of phantom listeners 'that dwelt in the lone house'. They are listening 'to that voice from the world of men'. They must be ghosts, among the moonbeams on the stair. The Traveller begins to feel uneasy 'he felt in his heart their strangeness'. Then he speaks again, saying, 'I kept my word'. His visit is as mysterious as the house full of ghosts. We feel the strangeness of the scene, heightened by the words 'from the one man left awake'. What had happened to the others? Why had the Traveller been forced to return? He mounts his horse, with plunging hoofs he is gone. The mystery is increased because the Traveller is given no name; there is little description in the poem. We are staring at objects in the shadows. The poet tells a part and leaves the rest, the mystery, to grow in our imaginations.

Read the poem again.

FLANNAN ISLE: W. W. GIBSON (p. 219)

AIM. To consider the mystery and appreciate the imaginative way the story is told.

INTRODUCTION. Read the poem. Ask for possible explanations of the mystery. Read the poem again.

DISCUSSION

Why did the three men sail to Flannan Isle? Because they had been told by a passing ship at dawn that:

> 'Though three men dwell on Flannan Isle
> To keep the lamp alight,
> As we steer'd under the lee, we caught
> No glimmer through the night.'

What kind of a day is it when the men set out to investigate? A bright sunny day; they sail without any sense of foreboding.

When do they begin to feel uneasy? As they draw near 'the lonely Isle'. The lighthouse towering white looks 'so ghostly in the cold sunlight'. They are struck 'with wonder all too dread for words'.

What increases their rising dread? They see 'three queer, black, ugly birds' too big for guillemot or shag, birds they would expect

to see, these looked 'like seamen sitting bolt-upright', they plunged from sight—
        'Without a sound, or spurt of white'.

There was an old superstition that the spirits of drowned sailors took the form of sea-birds.

The door of the lighthouse 'gaped...ajar'. On the threshold they smell the familiar limewash and tar which now has 'the strange scent of death'. By now they are all thoroughly frightened.

What is unusual in the living-room? The meal is untouched. A chair lies tumbled on the floor. A bird starves on its perch. Something, however, makes them catch their breath. They feel that something mysterious has happened, for the rock had been the death of others.

What lines express the terror of the three men?

> 'Each wishing he were safe afloat,
> On any sea, however far,
> So it be far from Flannan Isle.'

> 'And each with black foreboding eyed
> The door, ere we should fling it wide,'

> 'And stole into the room once more
> As frighten'd children steal.'

> 'And, as we listen'd in the gloom
> Of that forsaken living-room—
> A chill clutch on our breath—' ·

> 'Like curs, a glance has brought to heel,
> We listen'd, flinching there.'

What suggestions can you put forward as to the fate of the lighthouse keepers? These suggestions must be supported by evidence from the poem.

THE ETERNAL THEME

INTEGER VITAE: THOMAS CAMPION (p. 229)

AIM. To appreciate the quiet sincerity of the poet and the music of the verse.

INTRODUCTION. This poem is an adaptation of the Ode by the Latin poet Horace, *Integer vitae scelerisque purus*. The first line:

'The man of life upright'

is an adequate translation of the title of Campion's poem.

Read the poem asking for general comments on first impressions. Read the poem again.

DISCUSSION. This poem, based on a Latin Ode, is lyrical in movement. The Elizabethan age was the golden age of music as well as of poetry. Songs were written to be sung. Later they were written for the pleasure of their own sound without any musical accompaniment. Such poems were known as lyrics and are recognized by their brevity and charming sound.

What is the thought expressed in this poem? That the man of upright life knows contentment and peace of mind here on earth.

How are we made to feel the poet's sincerity? We feel and appreciate the poet's sincerity by his choice of words and by his skilful ordering of the rhythm by the arrangement of those words. We are compelled by the tone to read the poem slowly and seriously and this makes us conscious of the deep and real feeling of the poet. The stresses are carefully distributed so that the poem has a slow gentle rhythm:

> The man of life upright,
>> Whose guiltless heart is free
> From all dishonest deeds,
>> Or thought of vanity;

The man whose silent days
In harmless joys are spent,
Whom hopes cannot delude,
Nor sorrow discontent.

Notice the gentle flow of the sense through the first three stanzas. The fourth stanza is the most vigorous, rising to a climax of feeling in the lines

'The horrors of the deep
And terrors of the skies.'

After this the poem ends quietly with the quiet sounds of the words suiting exactly the calm assurance of the statements made

He makes the heaven his book,
His wisdom heavenly things;

and

The earth his sober inn
And quiet pilgrimage.

Read the poem again.

TO DAFFODILS: ROBERT HERRICK (p. 230)

AIM. To appreciate the delicate charm of this poem and something of its deeper meaning.

INTRODUCTION. Read the poem. Read Wordsworth's poem *The Daffodils*. Ask what immediate differences can be seen. Wordsworth's is a joyful poem. Herrick's is full of sadness at the passing of beauty.

DISCUSSION

What is the theme of the poem? The poet considers the beauty of the daffodils, and is sad to think how soon they will fade and die. This leads him to think of the transience of human life. This, of course, is the theme of many poems; what is interesting here is the handling of the theme.

137

What kind of poem is this? It is a lyric or song. Its particular charm is due to the delicate pattern of sound. The sad music is achieved by the careful choice of simple, monosyllabic words with long vowel sounds. The ebb and flow of the lines is a feature of the poem; notice particularly the effective use of the two short lines in each stanza; the arrangement of the lines in stanza form creates many pauses which help the slow sad movement.

> Fair Daffodils, ‖ we weep to see
> You haste away ‖ so soon: ‖
> As yet the early-rising Sun
> Has not attain'd his noon. ‖
> Stay, ‖ stay, ‖
> Until the hasting day ‖
> Has run
> But to the even-song; ‖
> And, ‖ having pray'd together, ‖ we
> Will go ‖ with you along. ‖

Read the poem again to show how the carefully chosen words are set in their phrases and the phrases in the poetic pattern with the delicate skill reminding us of the jeweller's art.

VIRTUE: GEORGE HERBERT (p. 233)

AIM. To appreciate the music and to consider the emotion that inspired the poem.

INTRODUCTION. Read the poem slowly and quietly. Read the poem again and ask for general comments on first impressions.

DISCUSSION

What is the theme of the poem?

What emotion inspired this poem?

Show how the third stanza summarizes the first two and leads to the point of the poem in the last stanza.

The first stanza tells us how the day 'so cool, so calm, so bright' must pass 'For thou must die'.

The second stanza tells us how the rose for all its beauty must die.

The third stanza tells us that spring, full of sweet days and roses (which have been already mentioned), must also die. In fact all lovely things must die. Then comes the great affirmation in the last stanza:

> 'Only a sweet and virtuous soul
> Like season'd timber, never gives;
> But though the whole world turn to coal,
>   Then chiefly lives.'

The thoughts from the beginning have been leading up to the statement in the last stanza.

Never gives, means never yields, however heavy the pressure may be.

Turn to coal: turn into fuel; this is a reference to the day of judgment.

Consider carefully the pattern of the verse.

Though the poem appears to be simple, it is the simplicity that conceals art. It is most carefully constructed and is full of subtle emphases. The tone is calm and serene, the movement slow and controlled. The exquisitely chosen words, with long vowel sounds and muted consonants, the pauses and varied rhythms make the poem an achievement of art as well as of feeling.

Note how the rhythm varies from the normal iambic line

> The dew shall weep thy fall to-night

in the other lines in the poem.

> Sweet day, so cool, so calm, so bright!
> The bridal of the earth and sky.

This variation from the norm gives the verse its exquisite cadence.

Notice how in the fourth stanza the positive statement of faith rises to a climax in the strong stresses of the last line:

> Only a sweet and virtuous soul
> Like season'd timber never gives;
> But though the whole world turn to coal,
>   Then chiefly lives.

The seventeenth-century poets have been praised as 'masters of the "neutral style", of a diction equally appropriate, according as it may be used, to prose and verse'. *What do you notice about the diction used in this poem?*

The diction may be called domestic. The poet talks of a 'box where sweets compacted lie', of 'season'd timber', a world 'turned to coal'. The hue of the rose is 'angry and brave'. Such words are simple, everyday words and yet the poem does not lose its poetic quality and become prosaic.

A SLUMBER DID MY SPIRIT SEAL:
WILLIAM WORDSWORTH (p. 241)

AIM. To consider how we can be said to enjoy a sad poem.

INTRODUCTION. Read the poem with a word, perhaps, on the complete simplicity of diction. Read the poem again.

DISCUSSION. Mr Frank Kendon, in his *Adventure of Poetry*, in writing of this poem puts the question, 'How can we be said to enjoy or take pleasure from a poem that is a record of a man's breaking heart?' He goes on to say:

'Read Wordsworth's poem again and again. It is impossible to deny the beauty of it: its briefness is so brave; the poem itself, in its shape and strength, is like the man it portrays, taking sorrow by both hands, holding on to it, getting the simple facts of it right and clear. And we take pleasure to perceive all this in the poem. There is beauty for us in a man's courage, and we admire it. But we recognize too in the plain statements of the poem the brave way the words are made fitting for the intensity of feeling portrayed, and we admire the self-restraint of the poet—we admire his power and take pleasure in the rightness of his judgement. More than this is in our pleasure too; perhaps something of his courage is given to us, and we take comfort from his example, just as something of his grief is felt by us, and we are glad that we can share it. These powers of entering into and sharing other feelings are always present (as it were asleep) in our minds; it is the poet's particular gift to be able to waken them with words. Our pleasure in poetry, it seems to me, is of a double nature: we enjoy having these powers of sympathy and feeling wakened and exercised, and we enjoy the degree of skill with which words are used, by the poet, to that end.'

Though the poem is so short, and the diction (with the exception of the one word 'diurnal') so simple, it is one of the finest of English lyrics. The first line:

'A slumber did my spirit seal'

with its modulated vowels and sibilant 's's' suggests something of a trance-like state, the unexpected word 'seal' hinting at secrecy. In the next line:

'I had no human fears'

the word 'human' is contrasted with the word 'spirit' in the preceding line and with 'thing' in 'She seemed a thing that could not feel'. The word 'thing' suggests an inanimate object beyond the effects of time and change. Against this thought of her as inanimate plays the word 'touch', 'the touch of earthly years'. We have the interplay of key-words in the stanza, 'spirit' and 'human', 'thing', 'touch' and 'earthly'.

She is now dead. The unthought-of change has taken place. She was alive. Now she has 'no motion, no force'. The poet seems numbed by his loss for he felt so secure, 'he had no human fears'. He must accept what he thought could never happen. He does this both with humility and controlled anguish. It is his acceptance which gives force to his utterance; nothing can mitigate his loss:

'No motion has she now, no force;
She neither hears nor sees.'

Yet, he thinks, she is now one with nature; to emphasize this she becomes one with the turning globe:

'Rolled round in earth's diurnal course,
With rocks, and stones, and trees.'

'Diurnal' is a latinized word, which by sound and meaning gives the wide-sweeping motion of the earth. She is rolled round impassively now (where once she 'could not feel the touch of earthly years') with rocks, and stones, and trees. Notice the lightening in sound (and in association) in the last line—from the harsh weight of 'rocks' to the softer sound of 'stones' and thence to 'trees', with its change from the completely inanimate, 'rocks and stones', to the 'trees', rooted yet living in the earth. Here the poet may be suggesting a kind of existence in the universe of which she is now a part.

The grief of the poet has been transmuted into a stoical acceptance which finds perfect expression in eight short lines of poetry. And as we read the poem we enjoy it.

PROSPICE: ROBERT BROWNING (p. 242)

AIM. To appreciate the vigour of the poem and the analogy between going on a dangerous journey and facing death.

INTRODUCTION. Explain that the poem was written a short time after the death of the poet's wife, and that it expresses the poet's feelings on facing death, and, after death, joining his wife.

Read the poem bringing out the strong compelling rhythms. Ask for general comments before reading the poem a second time.

DISCUSSION

What is the theme of the poem? The poem opens with a challenging question, 'Fear death?' Death threatening on a dangerous journey, and the comparison between that journey and the facing of death is worked out through the poem.

How are the dangers of the journey presented? We have a series of vivid pictures described in words of rising intensity to the line:

'For the journey is done and the summit attained.'

Some of the images make us feel the sensations described: 'to feel the fog in my throat', 'the mist in my face'.

What lines describe the poet's courage?

'Yet the *strong* man must go.'
'I was ever a *fighter*, so—one fight more,
    The best and the last!'
'No! let me taste the whole of it, fare like my *peers*
    The *heroes* of old.'
'For sudden the worst turns the best to the *brave*,
    The black minute's at end.'

142

Where does the poet ask that his difficulties be not reduced?

> 'I would hate that death bandaged my eyes, and forbore,
>   And bade me creep past.'
> 'No! let me taste the whole of it.'
> 'Bear the brunt.'

What encourages him in his determination to endure? His belief that 'the worst turns the best to the brave' that through his endurance shall suddenly come 'first a peace out of pain, then a light'.

What is the poet's final reward? Reunion with his wife, and rest with God.

What gives the poem its vigour? The obvious sincerity of the poet's feelings; the choice of short expressive words; the variation of long and short lines and the use of heavy stresses with a staccato effect and rising intensity.

> Fear death?—to feel the fog in my throat,
>   The mist in my face,
> When the snows begin, and the blasts denote
>   I am nearing the place,
> The power of the night, the press of the storm,
>   The post of the foe.

Read the poem again.

UP-HILL: CHRISTINA ROSSETTI (p. 243)

AIM. To appreciate the simplicity of the poem and understand its secondary meaning.

INTRODUCTION. Read the poem to the class.

DISCUSSION. Dr Jagger, in his *Poetry in School*, has some illuminating comments to make upon this poem.

'On the surface, this poem is a dialogue between a traveller and another. There is no explicit hint that it has any other meaning. But anyone who left it with the belief in his mind that this was all that it was intended to convey would miss the inspiration of the poet. Underneath the superficial or primary meaning of the words, which is trivial, is a secondary meaning which contains the real inspiration.

'It would be difficult to imagine any set of words which would convey the mood of the writer more perfectly than *Up-Hill*, and more delicately. It is not only behind the subject-matter, or story, that the secondary meaning lies hidden. All the form of the piece is directed to the same end. The metre, and the arrangement of the lines, are chosen to suggest the same melancholy reflectiveness. Very often there is no secondary meaning behind the subject-matter of a poem; but, nevertheless, most poems have an implicit meaning which is conveyed by the poetic form. In Lord Macaulay's *Horatius*, which is as plain and as straightforward as the most matter-of-fact reader could wish, the martial feeling and excitement are induced by the rapid metre as much as by the subject-matter of the tale. In both these poems, the poet has had recourse to indirect means in order to suggest his meaning; and he was compelled to do so, because he could not suggest it so powerfully, if at all, by direct means.

'In *Up-Hill*, we may say that delicacy of feeling shrinks from a direct expression, and that the poet throws a veil over her feelings in the allegory she employed. But a veil challenges the imagination, and may result in a greater degree of revelation than a direct statement. It is in such ways that the method of poetry becomes a more powerful and subtler method of communication than the direct methods of ordinary life. A poet writes to himself as much as to others, and finds in metre and rhyme, and in figures, an actual aid to expression, not a hindrance. He is willing to trust to their care feelings and imaginations which he would have been chary of setting before himself in the harsh directness of prose, even if he had been able.

'What, then, is the subject of Christina Rossetti's poem? Though it is, superficially, a dialogue between a traveller and another person, the most important part of the subject lies beneath the surface, and we have just seen that this could not be expressed as adequately in any other way. If it could be done, the allegory would be unnecessary, and the poem, instead of being an inspired vision, would be an artificial combination of two parallel ideas. The entire words of a poem are the only words in which its meaning can be fully stated. The meaning of a poem can only be apprehended intuitively; it cannot be comprehended, nor formulated. The whole poem is its own subject; an abstract definition, not being art, can be only part of the poet's meaning.'

What is the underlying meaning of the line

'You cannot miss that inn'?

Explain 'Of labour you shall find the sum'.
What is meant by 'Yea, beds for all who come'?
Read the poem again.

FIDELE: WILLIAM SHAKESPEARE (p. 247)

AIM. To appreciate the lyrical beauty of this poem.

INTRODUCTION. Read the poem to the class.
Give briefly the situation in *Cymbeline* leading to this song.

The heroine Imogen has been cruelly wronged and runs away from the court of her father, Cymbeline, disguised as a boy with the name Fidele. In her wanderings in Wales she is befriended by Guiderius and Arviragus. They are really her two brothers who have been stolen when tiny children from their parents. Naturally they do not recognize each other but are strangely attracted. One day Imogen feels sick and swallows a drug which she carried with her. She falls into a deep sleep, is thought to be dead, and the two brothers sing this dirge.

DISCUSSION. The mood and feeling of the poet is here given perfect lyrical utterance. This is achieved by the combination of sense, sound and suggestion. It is impossible to explain how Shakespeare fuses these to create his mood but we can feel that he has done so. The mood here is one of quiet resignation, of acceptance of the inevitability of death; this is conveyed as much by the music of the words and the movement of the verse as by the meaning.

The movement of the verse is trochaic and this helps to give the poem its heavy sadness.

Fear no more the heat o' the sun,
Nor the furious winter's rages;

Thou thy worldly task hast done,
Home art gone, and ta'en thy wages:
Golden lads and girls all must,
As chimney-sweepers, come to dust.

Notice the simplicity of the images used: the 'heat o' the sun', the 'furious winter's rages', returning home having 'taken the wages' earned. Death is accepted naturally, the 'worldly task' completed. The use of the word 'golden' with all its romantic associations is arresting, and stands out strongly in contrast to the word 'chimney-sweepers'. The golden lads and girls, as chimney-sweepers, come to dust. Death comes to all and is an escape from the tyranny of the great, from the cares of everyday existence, from sudden violent disaster. (The thunder-stone is a thunder-bolt. It was believed that when a person was killed by lightning he was struck dead by a stone.) Death is an escape from slander and censure, from joy and pain. All lovers with their zest for life must 'consign to thee', that is, agree to accept the same contract with Death.

Death then has its consolations. Moreover, it is inevitable and universal, and Shakespeare says to us gently, 'Fear no more'.

APPENDIX: EXPOSITION OF SELECTED POEMS

DANIEL: VACHEL LINDSAY (I, p. 25)

This poem has also the title *The Daniel Jazz*. Jazz is a kind of syncopated dance-music with a ragtime rhythm introduced by American negroes. The poem is a kind of jazz version of the story of Daniel in the lions' den, based on the Book of Daniel, ch. vi. It is told as a simple American negro might relate the story.

Darius the Great, son of Hystaspes, was King of Persia 521–485 B.C. He greatly extended the Persian empire, and in his reign began the great war between the Persians and the Greeks. Darius is referred to in Daniel v and the following chapters.

Old man Ahab leaves his card

Ahab, son of Omri, King of Israel 875–82 B.C. His wife was Jezebel (see I Kings xvi).

Elisha and the bears are a-waiting in the yard

Elisha was a Hebrew prophet, the reputed successor of Elijah. He caused two she-bears to fall upon forty-two boys who insulted him (II Kings ii. 23–5).

Here comes Pharaoh and his snakes a-calling

Moses and Aaron cast down rods before Pharaoh, and the rods turned into serpents (Exodus vii. 9–13).

Here comes Cain and his wife a-calling

Cain was the first-born son of Adam and Eve. His wife, according to one legend, was Adah.

Shadrach, Meshach and Abednego for tea

These were the three Jews who passed unscathed through the fiery furnace in the reign of Nebuchadnezzar (Daniel iii).

Here comes Jonah, and the Whale

When Jonah was ordered to prophesy against Nineveh he sailed instead for Tarshish. The sailors threw Jonah into the sea because they thought him to be responsible for the storm. He was swallowed by 'a great fish' and thrown up again upon the land (Jonah i and ii).

Send Gabriel

Gabriel: one of the archangels (Daniel ix. 21 and St Luke i. 19).

THE CONGO: VACHEL LINDSAY (I, p. 27)

SECTION I

Fat black bucks in a wine-barrel room

'Bucks' refers to male negroes.

'Blood' screamed the skull-faced lean witch-doctors

Witch-doctors are negro magicians.

'Whirl ye the deadly voo-doo rattle'

Voo-doo rattle is one connected with witchcraft.

To the Mountains of the Moon

The River Congo rises in these mountains in East Africa.

Boom, kill the Arabs,
Boom, kill the white men

A reference to the part the Arabs and the white men played in the slave trade.

Listen to the yell of Leopold's ghost

Leopold II, King of the Belgians, who founded the Congo Free State, and treated the negroes with great brutality.

Or Mumbo-Jumbo, God of the Congo

Mumbo-Jumbo is a grotesque idol said to be worshipped by some negro tribes.

Mumbo-Jumbo will hoo-doo you

'Hoo-doo' means bring you bad luck.

148

SECTION II

> *Wild crap-shooters with a whoop and a call*

Wild gamblers with dice.

> *Danced the juba in their gambling-hall*

A high-spirited negro dance accompanied by shouts of 'juba'.

> *At the baboon butler in the agate door*

An agate is a semi-precious stone.

> *Came the cake-walk princes in their long red coats*

A cake-walk is a kind of strutting dance developed from negro contests in graceful walking, with a cake for the prize.

> *And the couples railed at the chant and the frown*

The couples shouted abusive language at the serious chanting and the frown of the magicians.

SECTION III

> *Starting the jubilee revival shout*

'Jubilee' means a season of rejoicing; when associated with religion it is connected with the idea of emancipation. At revival meetings negroes would express their religious fervour by shouting 'Halleluia!'

> *And sang of Jacob, and the golden stairs*

A reference to Jacob's Ladder, which he saw in a dream reaching to Heaven with angels ascending and descending (Genesis xxviii).

> *And showed the Apostles with their coats of mail*

According to tradition the twelve Apostles were represented as warriors in armour.

> *The vine-snared trees fell down in files*

Trees wrapped round with vines (or climbing plants) fell down in rows.

WEATHERS: THOMAS HARDY (I, p. 43)

And maids come forth sprig-muslin drest

Sprig-muslin is thin cotton material with a pattern of sprigs or flower-sprays on it.

And citizens dream of the south and west

A reference to the citizens of London and their dreaming of holidays on the south and west coasts of England.

When beeches drip in browns and duns

Dun is a dull greyish-brown colour.

And thresh, and ply

The movement of the branches of the beech trees suggests the sound of a threshing machine and of the wooden arms of a weaving machine ('ply').

And hill-hid tides throb, throe on throe

And the sea ('tides') though it is hidden behind the hill can be heard moaning as though in pain. ('Throe' means anguish.)

ROBIN HOOD AND LITTLE JOHN: TRADITIONAL (I, p. 61)

Robin Hood is a legendary figure, though the claim is made that his real name was Fitzooth, and that he was the Earl of Huntingdon. He was first mentioned by Langland in *Piers Plowman* about 1377. He is next referred to by Andrew of Wyntoun in his *Original Chronicle of Scotland*, written about 1420. The Robin Hood ballads date from the thirteenth century; one, *A Lytell Geste of Robyn Hode*, was first printed about 1510.

The Robin Hood story has probably some historical basis. Langland suggests that he was contemporary with Randle, Earl of Chester, who flourished in the reigns of Richard I, John and Henry III. By the first half of the fourteenth century the legend is firmly established. Just as King Arthur was popular with the upper classes, so Robin Hood became the hero of the ordinary people. He was the ideal yeoman. He robs the rich to endow the poor. He hates monks and abbots. He defies the sheriff. He is a great sportsman, a superb archer, lover of the greensward and the free life out of doors. He is above all brave and adventurous. The story is localized between Barnsdale in Yorkshire and Sherwood Forest in Nottinghamshire.

Robin Hood's chief companions were Little John, William Scadlock (or Scarlet), George Green the pinder (or pound-keeper) of Wakefield, Much a miller's son, Tuck a friar, and one woman named Marian.

These ballads, *Robin Hood and Little John* and *Robin Hood and the Widow's Three Sons*, are good examples of the Robin Hood cycle.

THE RAINBOW: WILLIAM WORDSWORTH (I, p. 85)

Wordsworth was probably thinking not only of the beauty of the rainbow but of its religious associations (Genesis ix. 12–17).

The Child is father of the Man

This paradox means that those qualities which appear in the man have been lying dormant in the child.

And I could wish my days to be
Bound each to each by natural piety

If the poet is giving weight to the word 'piety' in the Latin sense of reverence due to parents, then the lines probably mean 'such reverent affection as is felt by the child for its parent ought to be felt by the mature man for the days of his own childhood'. It is, however, more probable that he means by natural piety, 'a reverent affection for Nature'. Wordsworth's attitude to Nature was conditioned by his idealism. We find him projecting his own feeling of well-being into the external world and finding it good. Nature is then 'the norm' to which man must return to be blessed. Hence his desire that his days should be linked together by this reverent affection for Nature.

A BIRTHDAY: CHRISTINA ROSSETTI (I, p. 87)

Whose nest is in a watered shoot

The imagery throughout this poem reminds one of Eastern literature. The tree in which the bird builds its nest is 'planted by the water-side'.

That paddles in a halcyon sea

The halcyon is the kingfisher. There was an ancient belief that there was a calm at sea during the fourteen days in winter when the kingfisher was breeding.

Hang it with vair and purple dyes

Vair is a kind of fur, known as one of the heraldic furs. Vair may be used here in its heraldic sense of particoloured.

In leaves, and silver fleurs-de-lys

Fleur-de-lys, the heraldic lily (best known from having been borne upon the royal arms of France).

TO THE CUCKOO: WILLIAM WORDSWORTH (I, p. 87)

O blessèd Bird! the earth we pace
Again appears to be
An unsubstantial, faery place,
That is fit home for Thee!

This poem is visionary throughout; but it is not ecstatic, it has no religious implication. As J. C. Smith says:

Vision is neither dream, nor hallucination, nor reverie. These are all subjective states, mere phantasies of our own creation, which bring us no knowledge of anything beyond us: in vision we perceive something not ourselves. So much all visionaries affirm; but when we press for a more positive account of their experience they fall back on metaphor. In vision, they tell us, a momentary transparency comes over the external world, revealing its inner constitution. Or the senses, they say, are laid asleep, and we see into the life of things; as if, there being in ordinary perception four terms —soul: sense: nature: reality—in vision the middle terms are for

152

a moment cancelled, and the extremes communicate directly. Or again, the world seems to melt into the soul, to become a dream, a prospect in the mind, as if all things were within the self.

It is only in such terms as these that we can explain what the poet means when he says that the earth appears to be 'an unsubstantial faery place'.

THE DARKLING THRUSH: THOMAS HARDY (I, p. 88)

This poem was written on the last day of the nineteenth century. The winter landscape is likened to the corpse of the century, and the pervading gloom is in keeping with the poet's feelings.

The tangled bine-stems scored the sky

The tangled stems of climbing plants ('bine') seemed to draw lines across the sky.

And all mankind that haunted nigh

And all the people who lived in that neighbourhood.

The land's sharp features seemed to be
The Century's corpse outleant

The image is that of the bareness of the countryside (sharpened by winter) likened to a corpse with the bones already more apparent (leaning or pushing out from the dead body).

The ancient pulse of germ and birth
Was shrunken hard and dry

The life force itself which stirs into creation was apparently dead.

Of joy illimited

'Illimited' means boundless.

THE VAGABOND: ROBERT LOUIS STEVENSON (I, p. 89)

This poem was written 'for an air of Schubert'.

Let the lave go by me

'Lave' is Scottish for 'all the rest'.

THE WOODLARK: GERARD MANLEY HOPKINS (I, p. 107)

Teevo cheevo cheevio chee

T. A. Coward in his book, *The Birds of the British Isles*, describes the song of the woodlark as follows: 'richer in tone than that of the skylark but less varied, mainly the repetition of two or three sweet notes. The call-note is double or triple, "tweedlie" or "too-lui-ie", and is often uttered in flight.'

To-day the sky is two and two
With white strokes and strains of the blue

Hopkins had a strong feeling for pied things. Here he describes the blue and white sky as though it had been painted in alternate strokes of white and blue. The word 'strains' suggests a 'trace' of blue, as one might say a strain or snatch of song.

And the braided ear breaks out of the sheath

The ear of wheat looks like roughly braided or plaited material. The sheath refers to the individual husks containing the ears of wheat.

The ear in milk, lush the sash

The ear of wheat, before it is ripe, contains a large amount of water. At this stage the grain is said to be 'in the milk'; on squeezing it yields a white liquid rather like milk in appearance. The sash is the 'beard' of the wheat which growing freely looks 'lush' or luxuriant.

The blood-gush blade-gash
Flame-rash rudred
Bud shelling or broad-shed

These lines describe a half-open poppy bud. The four vivid red petals are soft in texture, hence 'crush-silk poppies aflash', and Hopkins uses the violent imagery of blood gushing out from the wound gashed by a steel blade, and the ruddy flame-coloured rash of the bud 'shelling', that is bursting, or 'broad-shed' already fully open.

> *Tatter-tassel-tangled and dingle-a-dangled*
> *Dandy-hung dainty head*

The poppy flower nods, especially when in bud. When the petals begin to appear they are so soft and have been packed so tightly in the bud that they appear tattered and tangled. The flower stalk is so slender that the flower seems to dangle on a thread.

> *Sunspurge and oxeye*
> *And lace-leaved lovely*
> *Foam-tuft fumitory*

Sunspurge is a very common plant with yellow-green flowers and large, rather fleshy leaves. The oxeye, dog or moon daisy grows freely in pastures and on arable land.

The common fumitory is frequently seen growing, like its relative the poppy, in cornfields. The leaves are finely divided and look just like lace. The flowers are small and graceful. In one variety of the species the flowers are white ('foam-tuft') before pollination, afterwards they turn pink or carmine.

> *Through the velvety wind V-winged*

'Velvety' suggests the softness of the wind and the ease of the bird's flight as it ascends and descends in spirals. The wings of most birds are shaped like the letter V.

> *To the nest's nook I balance and buoy*

The nest of the woodlark is placed upon the ground and is usually well concealed, often under a low bush. The words 'balance' and 'buoy' give the floating movement of the bird before it settles on the ground in its nest.

RETURN OF SPRING: LORD TENNYSON (I, p. 118)

This is Section CXIV of *In Memoriam*, a long poem in which Tennyson mourns the death of his friend, Arthur Hallam.

Now the last long streak of snow disappears. Now every thicket of hawthorn begins to sprout with bursting buds round the square flower-beds, and the violets in heavy clusters come into flower round the roots of the ash trees.

Now the woodland echoes the sound of bird and beast. The distance in the clear air takes on a more beautiful colour, and the lark, lost in the throbbing blue of the sky, becomes a song from an invisible bird.

Now the sunlight shining through the moving branches dances on lawn and meadow. The flocks of sheep are whiter down in the valley. Every white sail seems to be even whiter in the spring on winding river or the sea in the distance, where the sea-gull calls, or dives into the sea which shines green in the sun. Now the happy birds that have migrated to other lands in the winter return to this country to build their nests and sit upon their eggs. Spring brings these birds from one land to another. In my heart spring begins to stir also. And my reawakening grief like an April violet (a symbol of faithfulness) buds and blossoms with the other spring flowers.

THE KINGFISHER: W. H. DAVIES (I, p. 121)

It was the Rainbow gave thee birth

In Greek mythology Iris was the goddess of the rainbow. She was the daughter of Thaumas (son of Pontus, the Sea) and Electra (daughter of Oceanus).

And, as her mother's name was Tears

The poet, fancifully, makes Tears (the shower of rain which precedes the formation of the rainbow) the mother of Iris.

THE HOLLOW WOOD: EDWARD THOMAS (I, p. 123)

The simple statement made in this poem seems to conceal an inner meaning. The poem reads as a factual description of a decaying wood. There is, however, the strong contrast between the goldfinch flitting in the sun outside, and the strange things happening inside the hollow wood. There is something sinister about a wood:

Where birds swim like fish—
Fish that laugh and shriek

and where dead and dying trees are only given a semblance of life
'by lichen, ivy and moss' which keep the trees 'evergreen' as if to
mock them in death. The trees themselves are spoken of as though
they were human beings in their suffering. They are half-flayed—
the bark is peeling off in strips—and dead 'on their knees', surrounded by 'dog's mercury and moss'. The associations of the name
'dog's mercury' (man and dog) reinforces the idea of the trees as
people. Although the poem describes the natural processes of
growth and decay there is also a sense of something unnatural, of
forces working against Nature itself. The goldfinch in the sun (with
its vivid name) stands for the natural world. Even this world has an
air of triviality and superficiality about it. The words 'flits', 'twits',
'thistletops' (meagre, flippant words) suggest a heartlessness towards the world *inside* the hollow wood—the unnatural world. Here
birds (able to claim kinship with the goldfinch) move in a gloom
whose density is like another element so that they swim like fish.
Birds also laugh and shriek, but, in so far as they swim like fish,
they are fish that laugh and shriek—oddly disturbing images.
Horror of this unnatural world is heightened by the description of
trees slowly strangled by the green parasites which still preserve the
false appearance of life.

The hollow wood is, then, the poet's heart filled with a sense of
failure and a strangling despair. The bright goldfinch coming from
the outside tells him of that other world of gay, superficial success.

THE FLYCATCHER: SYLVIA LYND (I, p. 123)

He has found the nest made in some other Spring
Between the wall and the tall creeper stem,
Old as the wall itself, a slender tree
(Perhaps one of Raleigh's earliest transplanting)

Sir Walter Raleigh began the series of adventures in the coloniza-
tion of Virginia in 1584. He brought back to this country not only

the potato and tobacco, but also the virginia creeper which is referred to here. The flycatcher commonly builds its nest in the twisted stems of this creeper, or against the wall.

MALLARD: REX WARNER (I, p. 124)

Mallard or wild duck is the most abundant and best-known duck in Britain. *Squawking they rise from reeds into the sun*

It is usually not until the evening that 'flighting' takes place. Then in couples, for the Mallard pairs for life, the birds go off to the ponds, ditches or mud flats to seek food, returning at dawn. These birds are described rising from reeds into the evening sun.

climbing like furies, running on blood and bone

Describing the flight of the mallard, T. A. Coward says, 'The bird springs clear of the water, shooting upwards; the flight is swift, the wing-beats, rapid and strong, produce a swishing whistle'.

and sound their horns again

The cry of mallard is very similar to the sound of a motor horn. Seebohm spells the male note *quork*, and the female *quark*.

Suddenly siding to a bank of air unbidden
by hand signal or morse message of command
downsky they plane

Suddenly, without any visible sign or word of command, they turn sideways as though skirting the edge of a solid bank (of air) and move like planes down the sky.

till, with few flaps, orderly as they left earth,
alighting among curlew they pad on mud

The mallard, when about to alight, comes down with head well forward, with body upright checking its flight with a few movements of wing and tail. Mallard seeks mud-flats for its food, animal or vegetable, for it is omnivorous, is sifted from the mud which passes through its laminated bill. The curlew is a wading-bird which feeds day and night on sand and mud-flats.

LAPWING: REX WARNER (I, p. 124)

The poem opens with a description of autumn leaves blown by the wind. One image is heaped upon another; the leaves are 'spent coinage'; they are 'shuffled by heavy handed wind' like a pack of playing cards; they fly in the air like a swarm of insects, 'spent sunflies'; they drift like feathers, 'pinions of trees'. In the next verse, the flight of the lapwing, or green plover, is described. They are like flags in the autumn wind, blown about like the leaves. The lapwing is here called the minion (or darling or favourite) of the wind, 'the rush of air'.

> *companions of draggled cloud,*
> *tattered, scattered pell mell, diving, with side-slip suddenly wailing*
> *as they scale the uneasy sky flapping the lapwing fly*

The lapwing has broad round wings which flap slowly in flight; the bird moves fast, but without the dash of the sharp-winged wading-birds. They can fly high, 'companions of draggled cloud' and in autumn the flocks often indulge in aerial exercise, wild zigzag frenzy, wheeling and changing direction, as they rise and 'tremble up to cloud'. 'Suddenly wailing'—the ordinary call is a wheezy *pee-wee*, from which the bird gets the name 'Peewit'.

> *Plover, with under the tail pine-red, dead leafwealth in down displayed,*
> *crested with glancing crests, sheeny with seagreen, mirror of movement*
> *of the deep sea horses plunging, restless, fretted by the whip of wind*
> *tugging green tons, wet waste, lugging a mass to Labrador*

T. A. Coward describes the lapwing thus: 'the crown, crest, face, throat and breast of the male lapwing are black, the back and wings are metallic green glossed with bronze and purple; the sides of the neck and under parts below the breast are white. A broad black subterminal band crosses the white tail, and the upper and under tail-coverts are chestnut-red'. The crest of the lapwing turns green in autumn and there is no black on the throat. The poet describes the glancing crests 'sheeny with seagreen' and this leads to the image of the sea itself, with sea horses, urged by the whip of wind, dragging the green water to Labrador. Lapwings migrate, usually southwards.

An extraordinary weather migration took place at the end of December 1927. In an easterly gale large numbers of lapwings crossed the Atlantic and reached Labrador and Newfoundland.

> *with ever so much of forlorn ocean and wastes of wind*
> *in their elbowing of the air and in their lamentable call*

The flight of the lapwing and the long, undulating wild call suggest the stretches of desolate ocean and bleak spaces.

BAT: D. H. LAWRENCE (I, p. 125)

When under the arches of the Ponte Vecchio

The Ponte Vecchio is the Old Bridge in Florence.

Against the current of obscure Arno

The river Arno flows through Florence and then runs through the gorge of Golfolina to Empoli and Pisa. 'Obscure' means not visible (in the gorge).

Swallows with spools of dark thread sewing the shadows together

The swallows dart from one patch of shadow to another as they skim over the ground. This flight of the swallow is like thread spinning off the spool, and the image is completed with the thought that as the evening shadows extend and merge it is as though they were being sewn together.

> *A circle swoop, and a quick parabola under the bridge arches*
> *Where light pushes through*

This means a circular swoop, and a quick dipping curve of flight under the arches of the bridge where daylight can still be seen.

> *Dark air-life looping*
> *Yet missing the pure loop...*

The dark creature (or creature in the growing dark) at home in the air, looping easily, yet never performing the perfect loop of the swallow.

A twitch, a twitter, an elastic shudder in flight

This line catches perfectly the flight of the bat with wings of membrane not feathers, and its erratic movement.

Pipistrello!
Black piper on an infinitesimal pipe

'Pipistrello' means little piper and is Italian for bat. 'Infinitesimal pipe': the bat emits high-pitched cries continuously as it flies. Its hearing is keen especially for notes higher than those heard by the human ear. Solid objects reflect these sounds, warning the bat of obstacles; bats see fairly well but depend more on their hearing than sight to find food and to avoid collisions.

SNAKE: D. H. LAWRENCE (I, p. 126)

In the deep, strange-scented shade of the great dark carob-tree

The carob-tree, or locust-tree, is common in Mediterranean countries. The pods are eaten by men and animals, and are called St John's bread. The carob is said to be the tree which yielded the honey eaten by John the Baptist. The leaves have an aromatic smell.

And I thought of the albatross,
And I wished he would come back, my snake

The reference is to the albatross in Coleridge's *Rime of the Ancient Mariner*. The poet shares the feeling of guilt which assailed the ancient mariner, and says that he also has something to expiate: a pettiness in giving way to his feelings of fear and hatred of the snake 'a king in exile, uncrowned in the underworld'.

HORSES ON THE CAMARGUE: ROY CAMPBELL (I, p. 129)

The silver runaways of Neptune's car
Racing, spray-curled, like waves before the wind

In Roman mythology Neptune is a sea-god with the attributes of Poseidon, who was lord of the sea; also of earthquakes and horses. He is represented as a dignified figure; his car was drawn by white horses.

They feel their Master's trident in their side

'Trident' is a dual allusion to the trident (probably a fish-spear) carried by Neptune, and that carried by the guardians or cowboys of the Camargue.

HELEN OF KIRCONNELL: TRADITIONAL (I, p. 150)

In his 'Border Minstrelsy' Sir Walter Scott gives the following account of the incident on which this ballad is founded:

A lady of the name of Helen Irving, or Bell (for she is disputed by the two clans), daughter of the laird of Kirconnell, in Dumfriesshire, and celebrated for her beauty, was beloved by two gentlemen in the neighbourhood. The name of the favoured suitor was Adam Fleming, of Kirkpatrick; that of the other has escaped tradition, although it has been alleged that he was a Bell of Blacket-house. The addresses of the latter were, however, favoured by the friends of the lady, and the lovers were therefore obliged to meet in secret, and by night, in the churchyard of Kirconnell, a romantic spot surrounded by the river Kirtle. During one of these private interviews, the jealous and despised lover suddenly appeared at the opposite bank of the stream, and levelled his carbine at the breast of his rival. Helen threw herself before her lover, received in her bosom the bullet, and died in his arms. A desperate and mortal combat ensued between Fleming and the murderer, in which the latter was cut to pieces. The graves of the lovers are still shown in the churchyard at Kirconnell.

JOCK OF HAZELDEAN: SIR WALTER SCOTT (I, p. 157)

Young Frank is chief of Errington,
And lord of Langley-dale

Errington is in Northumberland; Langley-dale is near Barnard Castle, in the county of Durham.

Nor mettled hound, nor managed hawk,
Nor palfrey fresh and fair

'Mettled' means spirited ('the allusion is to the temper of the *metal* of a sword-blade', Skeat). 'Managed' means well-trained (manage: to handle). A palfrey is a saddle-horse.

The kirk was deck'd at morning-tide

The church was decorated in the morning ('tide' means 'time', coming from the same root).

They sought her baith by bower and ha'

A bower is, here, an inner appartment; a lady's private room.

LOCHINVAR: SIR WALTER SCOTT (I, p. 158)

This ballad appears in *Marmion*, canto V. It is founded on an old ballad, *Katharine Janfarie*, in which, however, it is the 'craven bridegroom' who is called Lochinvar.

He swam the Esk river where ford there was none;
But ere he alighted at Netherby gate

Netherby Hall, in Cumberland, is on the Esk, near the Scottish border.

That never a hall such a galliard did grace

A galliard was a lively dance for one couple only.

'She is won! we are gone, over bank, bush and scaur'

Scaur is a steep bank of bare earth formed by a river eating away the base.

There was racing and chasing, on Cannobie Lee

Cannobie is a border village in Eskdale, about fifteen miles north of Carlisle.

LORD ULLIN'S DAUGHTER: THOMAS CAMPBELL (I, p. 160)

This poem tells a true story. The graves of the two lovers, on which lie oblong slabs of stone, mark the place where the bodies were washed ashore.

Lord Ullin was Laird Allan MacLean, the owner of Knock at the head of Loch-na-Keal. Lochgyle is another name for Loch-na-Keal, on the west coast of Mull. The lovers were trying to reach Ulva, a small island off the west coast of Mull opposite the mouth of Loch-na-Keal. The shortest crossing was by Ulva Ferry to the north. This would have meant a long ride from Knock through hilly country where they would have been overtaken. Instead they chose the route from Knock to Gribun Ferry on the south side of the loch. This meant a much longer and more dangerous crossing.

> *By this the storm grew loud apace,*
> *The water-wraith was shrieking*

A water-wraith was a spirit which was supposed to appear above the surface of the water before a person was drowned.

HENRY HUDSON'S VOYAGE: DOROTHY WELLESLEY (I, p. 161)

Henry Hudson was a distinguished English navigator and explorer in the reign of Queen Elizabeth ('the Queen of Westminster'). He was employed by the Muscovy Company, and later by the Dutch East India Company, to discover a short route to China by way of the North Pole. He made several voyages between 1607 and 1610, during one of which he explored the Hudson River. In 1610 he made his fourth attempt on the North-West Passage, and discovered the bay and strait which are also named after him. Early in 1611 his crew mutinied, and set him with his son and seven others adrift in a small boat among the ice floes. Nothing further was heard of him.

YOU THAT LOVE ENGLAND: C. DAY LEWIS (I, p. 176)

> *Clear arias of light thrilling over her uplands*

An aria is an extended song in three sections, common in eighteenth-century opera and oratorio. The natural scene is described in terms of music. Light moving over the uplands is as thrilling to the eye as clear-sung arias are to the ear.

> *Over the chords of summer sustained peacefully*

'Chords' suggest the harmony of the scene on a peaceful summer's day.

> *Ceaseless the leaves' counterpoint in a west wind lively*

Counterpoint is a melody added as accompaniment to a given melody. In a lively west wind the leaves provide a ceaseless complicated melody.

Blossom and river rippling loveliest allegro

The flowers and the surface of the river are rippling with gay movement ('allegro') in the wind.

And the storms of wood strings brass at year's finale

The storms at the end of the year are like the last movement of an instrumental composition when wood-wind, strings and brass combine in a storm of sound.

Can you not hear the entrance of a new theme?

The young poets of the middle thirties (conscious of the dynamic force of fascism and communism) realized that great social changes were inevitable, and hoped for a new brotherhood of man.

Know you seek a new world, a saviour to establish
Long-lost kinship and restore the blood's fulfilment

The failures of the existing system revealed in mass unemployment, 'cursed towns and devastated areas', led to the search for a new world—the socialists' dream. The saviour (Christ, Karl Marx) would establish the true brotherhood of man ('kinship', 'blood's fulfilment') which had been lost.

You who like peace, good sticks, happy in a small way

You who like peaceful occupations, playing golf or hockey or walking, easily contented.

Yet passing derelict mills and barns roof-rent
Where despair has burnt itself out—hearts at a standstill

A reference to the depression in the 1930's.

Submit to the visiting angel, the strange new healer

The poet (privately) writes: 'the "strange new healer" was the hope and invigoration which I at that time believed Communism to offer.'

You above all who have come to the far end, victims
Of a run-down machine, who can bear it no longer

Those who have suffered most because of the drift to disaster in Europe at this time.

Or against hunger, bullies and spies preserving
The nerve for action, the spark of indignation

A reference to those who passively resisted the rise of Fascism.

Need fight in the dark no more, you know your enemies.
You shall be leaders when zero hour is signalled,
Wielders of power and welders of a new world

At last the real enemies (the fascists) were being recognized. Those who now resisted them passively would become the active leaders when the struggle began, and would become the creators of a new world.

HOW SLEEP THE BRAVE: WILLIAM COLLINS (I, p. 179)

At the battle of Fontenoy, 11 May 1745, in the War of the Austrian Succession, the English soldiers with 'dogged courage' exposed themselves to a terrible fire, and their column was torn to pieces. At Preston Pans, 21 September 1745, and at Falkirk, 17 January 1746, the English troops were defeated by the forces of the Young Pretender (grandson of James II), who claimed the English throne. The ode may commemorate the English soldiers who fell in all these engagements.

The 'pilgrim' and the 'hermit' are eighteenth-century personifications; they are used here to give more reality to the abstract qualities: honour and freedom.

MEN OF ENGLAND: THOMAS CAMPBELL (I, p. 179)

Yours are Hampden's, Russell's glory,
Sydney's matchless shade is yours,

John Hampden (1594–1643), a Buckinghamshire squire, cousin of Oliver Cromwell, was imprisoned for refusing to pay the unjust tax of 'ship money' levied by Charles I. A leader of the Parliamentary party in the Civil War, he was killed at Chalgrove Field in 1643. Lord William Russell (1639–83) was an enthusiast for political liberty in the reign of Charles II, and supported the Exclusion Bill brought forward to exclude the Duke of York (afterwards James II) from the throne as he was a Roman Catholic. Algernon Sidney (Sydney) (1622–83) was a republican leader in the Civil War, and was later associated with Russell in opposition to Charles II. Both Russell and Sidney were executed on false charges of complicity in the Rye House Plot (1683). Thus they were 'martyrs' in heroic story.

IT IS NOT TO BE THOUGHT OF THAT THE FLOOD: WILLIAM WORDSWORTH (I, p. 180)

Roused though it be full often to a mood
Which spurns the check of salutary bands

These lines interrupt the development of the image of the river flowing to the open sea. They refer to feelings of freedom which are often roused to a mood which spurns beneficial restraint. The image of the river is resumed in the next line which then runs ('It is not to be thought') that this most famous stream (of British freedom) should perish in bogs and sands (in inactivity).

BERMUDAS: ANDREW MARVELL (I, p. 182)

The full title of this poem is *Song of the Emigrants in Bermuda*. The poet imagines that he hears some Puritan refugees from the Stuart tyranny singing praises to God as they row along the coast of an island in the Bermudas, 'safe from the storms' and prelates' rage' (Persecution of Archbishop Laud).

Where He the huge sea-monsters wracks,
That lift the deep upon their backs,
He lands us on a grassy stage

Where God destroys the huge sea-monsters (the whales) that seem to carry the sea upon their backs, he lands us safely on a grassy shore.

And does in the pomegranates 'close
Jewels more rich than Ormuz shows

God encloses within the pomegranates glowing seeds (sometimes used as necklaces) which are like richer jewels than those of Ormuz. Ormuz (or Ormus) is a narrow island in the Persian Gulf. It was once the rich market and treasure-house between Persia and India, diamonds being its chief merchandize.

But apples plants of such a price,
No tree could ever bear them twice

These are pineapples of such excellence that no tree could bear such fruit a second time. In fact, the pineapple is a plant, the single fruit taking about six months to ripen; the second crop is produced from shoots on the stem of the original plant.

And makes the hollow seas that roar
Proclaim the ambergris on shore

Ambergris is a wax-like substance, which, as its name tells, resembles grey amber. It has a wonderfully sweet smell, and was once used in cookery. It is disgorged by the sperm-whale and floats ashore in tropical seas.

He cast (of which we rather boast)
The Gospel's pearl upon our coast

Not only has God given them (the refugees) the riches of the island—eternal Spring, oranges, pomegranates, figs, melons, pineapples, cedars, ambergris—but now he has given them the Gospel's pearl, the Christian Faith as their most precious possession. This poem was probably inspired by Marvell's friendship with John Oxenbridge, formerly a minister in the Bermudas.

ULYSSES: LORD TENNYSON (I, p. 184)

The poem is based upon the legend, long after Homer's time, that Ulysses sailed from Circe's island westward beyond the Pillars of Hercules. The legend appears to be Dante's own invention, and comes in the *Inferno* (canto XXVI):

When I left Circe, who for a year and more kept me in seclusion near Gaeta, before Aeneas so named the spot, neither my fondness for my son, nor reverence for my aged father, nor the affection due which should have rejoiced Penelope's heart, could conquer in me the eagerness I had to gain experience of the world, and of the virtues and vices of mankind; but I put forth on the deep open sea with but a single ship, and with that small company, which had not deserted me. Both coasts I saw as far as Spain and Morocco, and I saw the island of Sardinia, and those other isles whose shores are washed by that sea. I and my companions were old and weary, when we reached the narrow strait where Hercules had set up his boundary-marks to prevent man from venturing farther; on my right hand I left Seville behind, and on the opposite side Ceuta had already receded from my view. 'O brothers,' I cried, 'you who through dangers innumerable have reached the West, grudge not to the too brief waking-time of our senses which still remains, to win, by following in the Sun's wake, knowledge of the uninhabited world. Think of your origin; you were not created to live the life of brutes, but to pursue virtue and knowledge. By this brief address I made my companions so eager for the voyage that hardly after that could I have restrained them; and turning our stern towards the morning we sped our mad flight with oars for wings, ever tending more and more to the south.

In his dramatic monologue, Tennyson expresses through the mouth of the aged Ulysses a desire to transcend the limits of humanity and to seek angelic knowledge and risk spiritual death. After his absence of twenty years Ulysses spends years of idleness in his kingdom of Ithaca. He is here imagined about to start on a new voyage beyond the extreme west of the then known world.

By this still hearth, among these barren crags

A reference to Ulysses' kingdom, the rocky island of Ithaca, off the western shores of Greece.

Matched with an aged wife

Penelope, the daughter of Icarius of Sparta.

I mete and dole
Unequal laws unto a savage race

I administer laws which are unjust.

> *Through scudding drifts the rainy Hyades*
> *Vext the dim sea*

The Hyades: a group of seven stars whose rising at the same time as the sun was supposed to bring rain.

> *Far on the ringing plains of windy Troy*

Ulysses was in the army of Agamemnon at the siege of Troy. His exploits are related in Homer's *Iliad*.

> *Life piled on life*
> *Were all too little, and of one to me*
> *Little remains; but every hour is saved*
> *From that eternal silence, something more,*
> *A bringer of new things*

Many lives added to other lives would be too short to undergo all experience. I have only one life, and that is nearly over. But each hour left to me is not only an hour saved from the silence of eternal death, but something more, a bringer of new experience.

> *For some three suns to store and hoard myself*

Ulysses thinks that he may have three more years to live.

> *That ever with a frolic welcome took*
> *The thunder and the sunshine*

You (my mariners) that always gave a light-hearted welcome to disaster or good fortune.

> *Not unbecoming men that strove with Gods*

In the Trojan War, as described by Homer, gods fought on both the Greek and Trojan sides.

> *It may be we shall touch the Happy Isles*

Hesperia, the land of the blest, to which the souls of the favourites of the gods were conveyed after death. Supposed to lie in the west; for the Greek poets the western land was Italy. The Roman poets gave the name to Spain.

And see the great Achilles, whom we knew

Achilles was a Greek warrior in the Trojan War, hero of the *Iliad*.

One equal temper of heroic hearts

We are men of equal courage and determination.

ROMANCE: W. J. TURNER (II, p. 5)

The romantic words Chimborazo, Cotopaxi, and Popocatapetl are the names of three volcanoes. Chimborazo and Cotopaxi are in Ecuador. Popocatapetl is near Puebla, in Mexico.

ELDORADO: EDGAR ALLAN POE (II, p. 7)

Eldorado means 'the gilded one', and was the name given to a fabulous country or city, 'The Great and Golden City of Manoa', which was believed by the Spaniards to exist between the rivers Orinoco and Amazon. Sir Walter Raleigh twice visited Guiana, as the spot indicated, and published a highly-coloured account of its enormous wealth.

PORTRAIT OF A BOY: STEPHEN VINCENT BENET (II, p. 7)

Here the Cross swung; and there, confronting Mars,
The Centaur stormed aside a froth of stars

The Southern Cross is a constellation in the southern hemisphere. Mars is one of the planets. The Centaur is a constellation named after the mythical creature, half horse, half man.

Within, great casks like wattled aldermen

Aldermen with double chins, flesh hanging under the throat like that on a turkey.

Decked out in crimson, gemmed with syenite

Syenite is a grey crystalline rock which shines in the sun like quartz.

'Doubloons!' they said. The words crashed gold

A doubloon was a Spanish gold coin, a double pistole, worth about a guinea.

LEPANTO: G. K. CHESTERTON (II, p. 12)

Lepanto was a naval battle fought in 1571 in the Gulf of Corinth where the forces of the Christian, or Holy League, led by Don John of Austria, half-brother of Philip II of Spain, defeated the Turks.

And the Soldan of Byzantium is smiling as they run

Selim II became Sultan of Byzantium (the former name of Constantinople) in 1567.

For the inmost sea of all the earth is shaken with his ships.
They have dared the white republics up the capes of Italy,
They have dashed the Adriatic round the Lion of the Sea

The Turkish fleet commanded the Mediterranean, defied the white republics of Italy, those on the sea coast, Genoa, Este and Romagna; and sailing up the Adriatic dashed these waters round Venice, the Lion of the Sea.

And the Pope has cast his arms abroad for agony and loss,
And called the kings of Christendom for swords about the Cross

Pope Pius V in 1570 called for help against the Turks, and on 25 May 1571 formed the Holy League with Spain and Venice.

The cold Queen of England is looking in the glass

Queen Elizabeth was notoriously vain, and 'cold' probably refers to her reluctance to marry.

The shadow of the Valois is yawning at the Mass

France was ruled by the House of Valois from 1328 till 1589. In 1571, Charles IX was king in name only, the real power being in the hands of his mother Catherine de' Medici.

From evening isles fantastical rings faint the Spanish gun

A reference to the islands in the west, the new world, conquered by the Spaniards.

And the Lord upon the Golden Horn is laughing in the sun

The Sultan secure in his power with his fleet in the Golden Horn, the harbour on which Byzantium is built.

Where only on a nameless throne a crownless prince has stirred,
Where, risen from a doubtful seat and half attainted stall

Don John was the natural son of the Emperor Charles V. His mother was Barbara Blomberg, daughter of a wealthy family of Regensburg. Though recognized by Philip II as a member of the royal family, Don John never occupied a throne.

Then the tuckets...

A flourish of trumpets.

Mahound is in his paradise above the evening star

Mahound is a name of contempt for Mahomet.

He moves a mighty turban on the timeless houri's knees

A houri is a nymph of the Mohammedan paradise.

Black Azrael and Ariel and Ammon on the wing

Azrael was the Angel of Death; Ariel, one of the angels cast out of heaven; Ammon, the Libyan Jupiter, so called because his temple was in the desert (Greek 'ammos', sand).

Giants and the Genii,
Multiplex of wing and eye,
Whose strong obedience broke the sky
When Solomon was king

The Genii were an intermediate race between angels and men. They ruled on earth before the creation of Adam. Solomon is supposed to preside over the whole race of genii, who fill the sky when flying to obey his summons. The name Solomon seems to have arisen from a confusion of names of similar sound. The chief of the genii was called a suleyman, which was corrupted into a proper name. Here Mahomet is summoning all these spirits.

And chase the Giaours flying night and day

A Giaour is an unbeliever, one who disbelieves the Mohammedan faith.
We have set the seal of Solomon on all things under sun

The seal of Solomon (Suleyman, the chief of the genii) was a magic symbol made of two interlaced triangles, forming a six-pointed star.

The voice that shook our palaces—four hundred years ago

This refers to the Third Crusade 1189–92, in which Richard I of England took a leading part.

It is he that saith not 'Kismet'; it is he that knows not Fate;
It is Richard, it is Raymond, it is Godfrey in the gate!

He, the crusader, does not say Kismet (fate) because he does not recognize fate, that is admit defeat, a reference to the eight crusades. Richard is Richard I (Cœur de Lion). Raymond is the Count of Toulouse. Godfrey is de Bouillon, Duke of Lower Lorraine. Raymond and Godfrey took part in the First Crusade which captured Jerusalem in 1099.

Bolt from Iberia!
Don John of Austria
Is gone by Alcalar

Don John of Austria, like a thunderbolt from Spain, has passed by Alcalar. Alcalá de Henares, an old walled town near Madrid.

St Michael's on his Mountain in the sea-roads of the north

St Michael, prince of the celestial armies, is supposed to have appeared on the hill, afterwards called St Michael's Mount, in Mount's Bay in Cornwall. St Michael is trying to rouse England and France, but these countries do not respond.

The North is full of tangled things and texts and aching eyes

This refers to the religious controversies in England and France during the sixteenth century.

And Christian killeth Christian in a narrow dusty room

A reference to the murder of Rizzio by the Earls of Morton and Lindsay at Holyrood in 1566; or to the murder of the Duke of Guise in 1563, during the Huguenot wars.

King Philip's in his closet with the Fleece about his neck

The Golden Fleece (La Toison d'Or) was a Spanish order of knighthood; the collar was of firestones and steels with the badge, the figure of a golden ram, suspended from it. In his closet in the Escorial, or at Madrid, Philip sat day after day reading, annotating and drafting dispatches.

And his face is as a fungus of a leprous white and grey
Philip's laborious devotion to his work led to his becoming 'pale and grey, lean and gouty'.

Booms away past Italy the rumour of his raid
Here 'rumour' means noise.

The Pope was in his chapel before day or battle broke
Pius V led a most ascetic life, rising before dawn each day for the chapel service. This chapel is 'the hidden room in man's house', and the 'secret window'.

They fling great shadows foe-wards, making Cross and Castle dark
The Turkish ships are so numerous that they overshadow the Christian ships ('Cross and Castle' are symbols of Christendom).

They veil the plumèd lions on the galleys of St Mark
The emblem of Venice was the winged lion with the head of a man.

They are lost like slaves that swat, and in the skies of morning hung
The stairways of the tallest gods when tyranny was young
The Christian captives chained to the oars in the Turkish galleys are lost like those slaves who laboured to build the stairways of the tallest gods rising into the sky when tyranny first began.

They are countless, voiceless, hopeless as those fallen or fleeing on
Before the high Kings' horses in the granite of Babylon
A reference to the sacred processional way paved with granite slabs when Babylon was partially rebuilt by Nabopolassar and his son, Nebuchadnezzar.

Thronging of the thousands up that labour under sea,
White for bliss and blind for sun and stunned for liberty
After the battle was won, from 'twelve to fifteen thousand Christian captives were released from labour at the Turkish oar'.

Cervantes on his galley sets the sword back in the sheath

Cervantes, the great Spanish writer, at the age of twenty-four took part in the battle of Lepanto. Though ill with fever he insisted on action, and 'was posted with twelve men under him in a boat by the galley's side. He received three gunshot wounds, two in the chest, and one which permanently maimed his left hand—"for the greater glory of the right", in his own phrase.'

Up which a lean and foolish knight for ever rides in vain

Don Quixote, the hero of Cervantes' satirical romance.

RIO GRANDE: SACHEVERELL SITWELL (II, p. 16)

The Rio Grande is the Rio de la Plata estuary between Uruguay and the Argentine.

They dance no sarabande

A sarabande is a slow and stately Spanish dance.

On the marble pavers with each colour laid in shares

On the marble paving-stones, or tiles, on which the colours form a pattern.

The Comendador and the Alguacil are there

Comendador is a Spanish knight-commander. Alguacil is a constable, police-officer.

Loud is the marimba's note

A marimba is a kind of xylophone.

And louder still the tympanum

More usually timpano (or timpani) a kettle-drum.

The plectrum and the kettle-drum

A plectrum is a small instrument made of ivory quill, horn, or metal for plucking the strings of the lyre, zither or mandolin.

ON THE COAST OF COROMANDEL: OSBERT SITWELL (II, p. 18)

The Coromandel Coast is the coast of south-east Madras, India.

> *Chorally, that coral coast*
> *Correlates the bone to ghost,*
> *Till word and limb and note seem one,*
> *Blending, binding act to tone*

There is play upon the words 'chorally', 'coral', 'correlates', continued in the relation of coral to bone, bone to limb; these related as sound ('choral'), bone ('coral') give meaning to the binding of act and tone.

> *Pirouette to peruqued air*

A pirouette is a ballet-dancer's spin round on one foot or on point of toe. Peruqued air is music such as that composed by Handel with the be-wigged dignity of the eighteenth century.

> *Saraband and rigadoon*

A saraband is a stately Spanish dance; a rigadoon is a lively French dance for two persons.

> *Bids them do a gay fandango*

A fandango is a lively Spanish dance. The 'nautch-dance' is an East Indian dance by professional dancing-girls.

NOW THE FULL-THROATED DAFFODILS:
C. DAY LEWIS (II, p. 25)

> *Call resurrection from the ground*
> *And bid the year be told*

The image is that of the daffodils (heralds of spring) here blowing trumpets (trumpet daffodils) to awaken the dead earth and tell the year that it is spring.

> *The first flush of spring*

'Flush' refers to the fresh growth of vegetation, and to the blush of the almond-tree ('turns pink').

Winds loll and gossip through the town
Her secret whispering

The storms of winter are over. The casual attitude of the winds is suggested by 'loll and gossip' as the winds become the 'secret whispering' of spring, telling of the great event ('the resurrection from the ground').

Down drowsy avenues he cries
A novel great affair

Birds are now singing down avenues (still sleepy with the effects of winter) and proclaim a new exciting happening.

Summer to coronation comes
Through waving wild hedgerows

Summer reaches its height when wild roses blossom in the hedges, crowning the year. The symbolism here is that of the rose, an emblem of England, suggesting royalty, and coronation.

To-day crowds quicken in a street

Signs of life begin to appear: crowds grow and walk more briskly (the quick and the dead) in the streets.

The fish leaps in the flood

The fish is the sign of fertility, leaping in streams flooded by the winter rains.

Look there, gasometer rises

Even the gasometer seems to grow in spring: with warmer weather less gas is used and so the gasometer rises.

For our love's luck, our stowaway,
Stretches in his cabin

For the happy outcome of our love like a stowaway on board ship stretches in the cabin (the growing vegetation stirs under the earth).

Our youngster joy barely conceived
Shows up beneath the skin

Several images are used here; the image of the child, 'love's luck' now our 'youngster joy barely conceived' is extended; the image of a young joy (in spring) now beginning to show itself (as a pregnancy is shown 'beneath the skin'); and the image of plants pushing their way through the soil.

> *Our joy was but a gusty thing*
> *Without sinew or wit*
> *An infant flyaway; but now*
> *We make a man of it*

Our youngster was a flighty infant, uncertain in behaviour, lacking strength or intelligence; but now the child has become a man. That is, the first signs of spring are wavering and uncertain, but the season grows steadily to the fullness of summer.

ODE TO EVENING: WILLIAM COLLINS (II, p. 27)

Throughout the ode, Evening and evening are distinct, and Collins's attention is divided between the two. Whole stanzas are given up to natural description, without the slightest immediate reference to Evening the person. At other times Evening is directly addressed, but rather frigidly and in terms which only in the most general way suggest a connexion with the objective facts; as 'chaste Eve', 'nymph reserved', 'maid compos'd', and 'meekest Eve'. In a few places the relation is more intimate, and the personification more imaginative, notably in

> *Prepare thy shadowy car*

and in

> *marks o'er all*
> *Thy dewy fingers draw*
> *The gradual dusky veil.*

But the person and the phenomena are never completely fused, as might have happened had Collins been wholly absorbed in picturing the scenes of the real world at evening time. Keats, in his ode *To Autumn* (II, p. 30), was thus absorbed in catching up into words the subtle spirit of the 'season of mists and mellow fruitfulness', and he has identified Autumn the person with autumn the season. Autumn in his poem is 'no sturdy matron with sickle and sheaf'.

She is the haunting spirit of the 'granary floor', the 'half-reaped furrow', and the oozing cider-press. She has no fixed body, but many incarnations, in which 'whoever seeks abroad' may catch glimpses of her very essence. In the *Ode to Evening* there is no such inner unity. Collins was at once describing the appearances of nature at his favourite hour of twilight and writing an ode to the personified spirit of the hour. The spirit was as real to him as the hour, and he would probably not have cared to identify the two.

If aught of oaten stop, or pastoral song

The conclusion of this clause begins in line 15 with the words, 'Now teach me, maid compos'd'.

With brede ethereal wove

Woven with embroidery of unearthly delicacy of substance. The third stanza recalls the following lines from *Macbeth*:

> *ere the bat hath flown*
> *His cloister'd flight, ere to black Hecate's summons*
> *The shard-borne beetle with his drowsy hums*
> *Hath rung night's yawning peal.*

and this line from *Lycidas*:

> *What time the grey-fly winds her sultry horn.*

> *For when thy folding-star arising shows*
> *His paly circlet, at his warning lamp*

A reference to Hesperus, the evening star, here called 'folding-star' because sheep were enclosed in their folds when the star rose.

> *And many a nymph who wreathes her brows with sedge,*
> *And sheds the fresh'ning dew*

Nymphs of the springs, rivers and lakes, known as Naiads, would wear wreaths made of sedge.

> *Or Winter, yelling thro' the troublous air,*
> *Affrights thy shrinking train,*
> *And rudely rends thy robes*

A figurative expression of the fact that the twilight in winter is short, evening quickly ('thy shrinking train') giving place to night.

So long, regardful of thy quiet rule,
Shall Fancy, Friendship, Science, smiling Peace,
Thy gentlest influence own

Collins suggests that the evening is the best time to write poetry ('Fancy', the powers of the Imagination), entertain friends, and study ('Science', knowledge; Latin: *scientia*, *scire*, to know).

POEM IN OCTOBER: DYLAN THOMAS (II, p. 32)

Dylan Thomas has this to say about his use of imagery: 'A poem by myself needs a host of images. I make one image, though "make" is not the word: I let, perhaps, an image be made emotionally in me and then apply to it what intellectual and critical forces I possess; let it breed another; let that image contradict the first, make, of the third image, bred out of the other two together, a fourth contradictory image, and let them all, within my imposed formal limits, conflict.'

The poem describes a walk on his thirtieth birthday and his recollections of former days.

It was my thirtieth year to heaven
Woke to my hearing from harbour and neighbour wood

It was on my thirtieth birthday that I woke to hear the sounds coming from the harbour and the neighbouring wood.

And the mussel pooled and the heron
Priested shore

(To hear the sounds coming from) the shore with its pools with mussels and the heron moving like priests.

The morning beckon
With water praying and call of seagull and rook
And the knock of sailing boats on the net webbed wall
Myself to set foot
That second
In the still sleeping town and set forth

The morning, and the water which seems to be praying, and the call of seagull and rook, and the knock of the sailing boats against the sea-wall covered with drying nets, all beckon me to come into the town that is still asleep and set out.

and the birds of the winged trees flying my name

He felt that even the birds in the swaying trees knew that it was his birthday.

And walked abroad in a shower of all my days

I walked out of doors full of memories of former days.

A springful of larks

Larks singing as though filled with the zest of spring.

Here were fond climates and sweet singers suddenly
Come in the morning

The singing of the larks and the blackbirds brought with them the feel of spring ('fond climates').

Pale rain over the dwindling harbour
And over the sea wet church the size of a snail
With its horns through mist and the castle
Brown as owls

He looks back down at the harbour now small in the distance. Rain is falling. The church is wet as though washed by the sea, and seen through the misty rain the church and the castle are brown.

But all the gardens
Of spring and summer were blooming in the tall tales
Beyond the border and under the lark full cloud

In his imagination he can see the gardens beyond the outskirts of the town blooming as though it were spring and summer, and blooming more splendidly ('in the tall tales', the exaggeration of memory), under clouds full of larks.

It turned away from the blithe country
And down the other air and the blue altered sky

The weather changed in the happy country of the imagination. Now he could see another day, and the blue sky of full summer.

> *Through the parables*
> *Of sunlight*
> *And the legends of the green chapels*

> *And the twice told fields of infancy*
> *That his tears burned my cheeks and his heart moved in mine*

In his imagination he can see a child (himself) walking with his mother enjoying fairy stories and stories of the Bible. The recollection of these experiences made him live through the joys and sorrows of childhood once again.

> *In the listening*
> *Summertime of the dead whispered the truth of his joy*

In the past, when the summer air itself seemed to listen, the boy whispered the reality of his joy to the natural objects round about him.

> *And the mystery*
> *Sang alive*
> *Still in the water and singingbirds*

And the mystery of that communion with nature was still with him today as he looked at the water and heard the birds singing.

> *And the true*
> *Joy of the long dead child sang burning*
> *In the sun*

As he recalls the past he revives that thrilling communion with nature which he had experienced as a boy.

> *It was my thirtieth*
> *Year to heaven stood there then in the summer noon*
> *Though the town below lay leaved with October blood*

It was my thirtieth birthday and I stood there in the high summer of recollected happiness though the trees in the town below me were covered with autumn leaves.

> *O may my heart's truth*
> *Still be sung*
> *On this high hill in a year's turning*

May I be able to express my true feelings again on this high hill a year from today.

183

THE OLD SHIPS: JAMES ELROY FLECKER (II, p. 46)

The poet writes of old ships that he imagines he has seen sailing in the Eastern Mediterranean. Tyre, or Sur, is a town on the coast of Lebanon. Famagusta is a seaport on the east coast of Cyprus. If one is approaching Famagusta from the east, then 'the hidden sun' is setting behind Cyprus and as it outlines the island as a black mass it also shines on the sea making it appear like a lake of fire.

> *The pirate Genoese*
> *Hell-raked them till they rolled*
> *Blood, water, fruit and corpses up the hold*

The Genoese pirates swept the ships from stem to stern with shot till they were riddled and the water poured into the hold. Then the cargo of fruit and the corpses of the crew floated on the surface.

> *But I have seen,*
> *Pointing her shapely shadows from the dawn*
> *And image tumbled on a rose-swept bay,*
> *A drowsy ship of some yet older day*

I have seen a much older ship sending her shapely shadows across the bay as the sun rises behind her, and sending her reflection rippling ('tumbled') on the surface of the water rose-coloured with the light of dawn.

> *(Fished up beyond Aeaea, patched up new*
> *—Stern painted brighter blue—)*

In the *Odyssey*, Aeaea is the island of Circe situated in the stream Oceanus. Odysseus spent a year on the island, then Circe directed him to consult Tiresias in Hades.

> *That talkative, bald-headed seaman came*

Odysseus (or Ulysses) is represented in the *Iliad* as good in counsel no less than in battle. The epithet 'bald-headed' is used because he was ten years at the siege of Troy and ten years exposed to a series of misfortunes before he reached Ithaca.

> *And with great lies about his wooden horse*

Odysseus and Diomedes were said to have taken Troy by the

stratagem of hiding soldiers in a huge wooden horse, offered as a gift to the goddess Pallas Athene. The Trojans dragged the horse within their walls, and the city fell.

> *I watched in vain*
> *To see the mast burst open with a rose,*
> *And the whole deck put on its leaves again*

The poet sees Odysseus' ship in imagination; in his excitement he looks to see it not merely restored—'stern painted brighter blue' —but as it must have been when it was new, but he watches in vain.

THE SPANISH ARMADA: LORD MACAULAY (II, p. 55)

Her crew hath seen Castile's black fleet beyond Aurigny's isle

Castile was the more important part of Spain, and here stands for the whole of Spain. Aurigny's isle is Alderney, one of the Channel Islands.

The beacon blazed upon the roof of Edgecumbe's lofty hall

Edgecumbe is a peak near Plymouth, the building upon it has a commanding view of Plymouth Hoe and the surrounding countryside.

Behind him march the halberdiers

These were soldiers armed with the halberd; this was a long pole surmounted with a battle-axe and spear point.

For there behoves him to set up the standard of her Grace

For there near the market cross it is incumbent upon him (it is his duty) to set up the standard of Queen Elizabeth.

And underneath his deadly paw treads the gay Lilies down

On the English royal arms of that day the lion, the emblem of England, appeared in the quartering above the lilies, the emblem of France.

So stalk'd he when he turn'd to flight on that famed Picard field
Bohemia's plume, and Genoa's bow, and Caesar's eagle shield

The reference is to the battle of Crécy fought in Picardy in 1346. Here Edward III defeated the French king, Philip VI. The King of

Bohemia, fighting for France, was killed at Crécy. His crest, the triple feathers, with the motto *Ich dien*, was adopted by the Black Prince, Edward's eldest son and Prince of Wales, who won his spurs in the battle. The archers on the French side were Genoese mercenary crossbowmen. 'Caesar's eagle shield' is a reference to the imperial eagle of the House of Austria, and the troops of the Holy Roman Empire serving with the King of Bohemia.

So glared he when at Agincourt in wrath he turn'd to bay

Agincourt was a battle fought in the north of France in 1415 when Henry V, after a number of forced marches, turned on the French and defeated them.

Our glorious SEMPER EADEM—*the banner of our pride*

The Latin motto meaning 'always the same' is the motto on the English royal standard.

From Eddystone to Berwick bounds, from Lynn to Milford Bay

From south to north, from east to west. Eddystone is a rock to the south of Plymouth; Berwick, south-east of Scotland; Lynn, King's Lynn in Norfolk; Milford Bay, Milford Haven in Pembrokeshire.

High on Saint Michael's Mount it shone

St Michael's Mount is in Mount's Bay, east of Land's End.

The fisher left his skiff to rock on Tamar's glittering waves

Tamar is a river in Cornwall and Devon which flows south to Plymouth Sound.

The rugged miners pour'd to war from Mendip's sunless caves

The sunless caves are the lead-mines in the Mendip Hills.

O'er Longleat's towers, o'er Cranbourne's oaks, the fiery herald flew.

Longleat a great sixteenth-century house in Wiltshire. Cranbourne is an abbey in the north of Dorset.

He roused the shepherds of Stonehenge, the rangers of Beaulieu

Stonehenge is the famous druid circle on Salisbury Plain. Beaulieu is a town on the borders of the New Forest in Hampshire. The rangers are the keepers of the forest.

And ere the day three hundred horse had met on Clifton down

Clifton down is high land just outside Bristol.

Till the proud Peak unfurl'd the flag o'er Darwin's rocky dales

The Peak is a mountain at the southern end of the Pennine chain. Darwin is a town in north Lancashire.

Till twelve fair counties saw the blaze on Malvern's lonely height

The Malvern Hills are in Worcestershire, just west of the Severn.

Till stream'd in crimson on the wind the Wrekin's crest of light

The Wrekin is a peak near Shrewsbury.

Till broad and fierce the star came forth on Ely's stately fane

Until the beacon shone bright and fierce as a star on the cathedral of Ely.

Till Belvoir's lordly terraces the sign to Lincoln sent

Belvoir House is in Leicestershire, about seven miles from Grantham.

Till Skiddaw saw the fire that burn'd on Gaunt's embattled pile

Skiddaw is one of the peaks in Cumberland. 'Embattled pile' means a building with battlements, and refers to Lancaster castle which was restored by John of Gaunt.

THE LOSS OF THE *ROYAL GEORGE*: WILLIAM COWPER
(II, p. 61)

Cowper wrote this poem when he heard that words were required to fit the melody of Handel's March from *Scipio*. He based it upon an actual disaster.

The *Royal George* of 108 guns sank in Portsmouth Harbour on 29 August 1782 while undergoing a partial careening. Cowper accepted the official explanation that the ship capsized as the following lines show:

> *Eight hundred of the brave,*
> *Whose courage well was tried,*
> *Had made the vessel heel*
> *And laid her on her side.*

In point of fact the bottom timbers of the ship were rotten and she sprang a leak, though Cowper knew nothing of this.

Kempenfelt was the admiral, and the *Royal George* was his flagship.

The line '*Weigh the vessel up*' refers to the proposal to salvage the ship. An attempt was made, and proved to be unsuccessful.

THE WAR SONG OF DINAS VAWR: T. L. PEACOCK (II, p. 65)

Dyfed is the old kingdom of Pembrokeshire.

THE BALLAD OF AGINCOURT: MICHAEL DRAYTON (II, p. 67)

At Caux, the mouth of Seine

Caux, 'commonlie called Kidcaux', says Holinshed, whom Drayton, like Shakespeare, follows. It was the district north-east of the mouth of the Seine.

And taking many a fort

The advance, though a daring feat, was hardly the triumphal progress here represented. According to Hume, Henry offered to exchange his conquest of Harfleur for free passage for himself and his army to Calais.

Which in his height of pride,
King Henry to deride...

Baron de Helly with two other French knights were sent to summon Henry to surrender, as we learn from a contemporary ballad.

Poitiers and Cressy tell

Crécy (1346) and Poitiers (1356) were English victories over the French during the Hundred Years War.

Than when our grandsire great,
Claiming the regal seat

Grandsire refers to Edward III. The term is equivalent to 'ancestor', Edward being the great-grandfather of Henry V, whose father, Henry IV, was the only son of John of Gaunt, fourth son of Edward III. Edward claimed the French throne through his mother Isabella, daughter of Philip IV of France.

The Duke of York so dread

Edward, Duke of York, was the son of Edmond of Langly, younger brother of John of Gaunt.

Excester had the rear

John Holland, Duke of Exeter and Earl of Huntingdon.

Well it thine age became,
O noble Erpingham,
Which didst the signal aim
To our hid forces

Holinshed says: 'These [the archers] made somewhat forward, before whome there went an old knight Sir Thomas Erpingham (a man of great experience in the warre) with a warder [truncheon] in his hand; and when he cast up his warder, all the army shouted, but that was a signe to the archers in the meadow, which therewith shot wholie altogither at the vanward of the Frenchmen.'

And forth their bilbos drew

Bilbos were swords from Bilboa. Just as the best bows were made from Spanish yew, so too the best swords came from Spain.

Down the French host did ding

'Ding' means to belabour with blows; to beat down.

Gloucester, that Duke so good

Humphrey, younger brother of the king, had been created Earl of Pembroke and Duke of Gloucester in 1414. He later became Regent during the minority of Henry VI.

Clarence, in steel so bright

Thomas, younger brother of Henry, though older than Humphrey, was created Earl of Albemarle and Duke of Clarence in 1412.

Warwick in blood did wade

Richard de Beauchamp, Earl of Warwick. In point of fact Drayton is wrong in supposing Clarence and Warwick to have been present at the battle. They had been sent home from Harfleur in charge of prisoners.

Upon Saint Crispin's Day

'The daie following was the five and twentith of October in the year 1415, being then fridaie, and the feast of Crispine and Crispinian, a day faire and fortunate to the English, but most sorrowful and unluckie to the French' (Holinshed).

1805: ROBERT GRAVES (II, p. 73)

'*The most bird-witted, unaccountable,*
Odd little runt that ever I did spy'

'Runt' is a contemptuous term for an undersized person. Nelson, as a young officer, was presented to the Duke of Clarence, afterwards William IV, who remarked that he appeared

...to be the merest boy of a captain I ever beheld; and his dress was worthy of attention. He had on a full-laced uniform; his lank un-powdered hair was tied in a stiff Hessian tail of an extraordinary length; the old-fashioned flaps of his waistcoat added to the general quaintness of his figure, and produced an appearance which parti-cularly attracted my notice; for I had never seen anything like it before, nor could I imagine who he was or what he came about. My doubts were, however, removed when Lord Hood introduced me to him. There was something irresistibly pleasing in his address and conversation; and an enthusiasm, when speaking on professional subjects, that showed he was no common being.

'*One arm, one peeper, vain as Pretty Poll*'

Nelson lost his right eye at Calvi in Corsica in 1794, and his right arm at Santa Cruz in 1797. Regarding his vanity, see the note above.

'*A meddler, too, in foreign politics*'

Nelson played a leading part in the politics of the kingdom of Naples during the years 1798–1800.

190

'And gave his heart in pawn to a plain moll'

A reference to Nelson's love for Emma, Lady Hamilton.

'We tried to box him down, but up he popped'

The Lords of the Admiralty did their best to prevent Nelson's promotion, but he popped up like a jack in the box.

'And when he'd banged Napoleon at the Nile'

In 1798 Nelson destroyed the French fleet in Abukir Bay (the Battle of the Nile).

'You've heard that Copenhagen "blind eye" story?
We'd tied him to Nurse Parker's apron-strings—
By G-d, he snipped them through and snatched the glory!'

As second-in-command to Admiral Parker, a man of very ordinary gifts, Nelson won a brilliant victory at Copenhagen in 1801. This engagement is famous for the incident when Nelson put his telescope to his blind eye and declared that he could not see Parker's signal ordering his withdrawal from the fight.

'Handsome enough. The seas are England's now'

Nelson's decisive victory at Trafalgar on 21 October 1805 gained for England the command of the seas.

'He made the whole Fleet love him, damn his eyes!'

Nelson was more than merely a tactically and strategically brilliant Commander; he was a born leader of men—and men of all types, for the common seamen trusted and venerated him as much as did his officers. Nelson called his officers his 'band of brothers'.

HOHENLINDEN: THOMAS CAMPBELL (II, p. 74)

Hohenlinden, a village in Upper Bavaria, twenty miles east of Munich, is celebrated for the victory gained there over the Austrians by the French and Bavarians under Moreau on 3 December 1800. The weather was appalling, snow and rain succeeding one another till the roads were almost impassable. On December 2nd, the

Austrians under Archduke John were brought to a standstill. The greater mobility of the French army enabled them to strike the decisive blow on the following day when a fierce engagement took place on the wooded hills opposite Hohenlinden.

WATERLOO: LORD BYRON (II, p. 75)

There was a sound of revelry by night

A ball given by the Duchess of Richmond on the eve of Quatre-Bras. Thackeray describes it in *Vanity Fair*:

There never was, since the days of Darius, such a brilliant train of camp-followers as hung round the train of the Duke of Wellington's army in the Low Countries, in 1815; and led it dancing and feasting, as it were, up to the very brink of battle. A certain ball which a noble Duchess gave at Brussels on the 15th of June in the above-named year is historical. All Brussels had been in a state of excitement about it, and I have heard from ladies who were in that town at that period, that the talk and interest of persons of their own sex regarding the ball was much greater even than in respect of the enemy in their front.

Within a window'd niche of that high hall
Sate Brunswick's fated chieftain

The Duke of Brunswick, who was killed at Quatre-Bras. His father, who had issued a famous manifesto against the French Republic, had been fatally wounded at Auerstädt in 1806.

He rushed into the field, and, foremost fighting, fell

He (the Duke of Brunswick) led the Brunswick contingent against Marshal Ney near Bossu wood.

If ever more should meet those mutual eyes

Who could guess if those eyes which were answering one another ('soft eyes look'd love to eyes which spake again') should ever more meet again.

And wild and high the 'Cameron's gathering' rose!
The war-note of Lochiel, which Albyn's hills
Have heard, and heard, too, have her Saxon foes

'Cameron's gathering' was the call to arms—the pibroch, played on the bagpipes—of the Highland clan whose chief was called Lochiel. Albyn's hills, that is Scotland, had heard this martial sound, as also had the Cameron's enemy, the English.

And Evan's, Donald's fame rings in each clansman's ears!

Evan, and Donald, his grandson, were heads of the Cameron clan who had been supporters of the Stuarts.

And Ardennes waves above them her green leaves

Actually it was the wood of Soignies, not the Ardennes.

Which her own clay shall cover, heap'd and pent

The other clay—the bodies of the slain—will be covered with earth heaped over and then pressed down.

AFTER BLENHEIM: ROBERT SOUTHEY (II, p. 82)

Blenheim is a village in Bavaria, where, in 1704, the Duke of Marlborough and his ally, Prince Eugene of Savoy, defeated the French and the Bavarians.

Yon little stream hard by

This refers to the Nebel which flows into the Danube near Blenheim.

HART-LEAP WELL: WILLIAM WORDSWORTH (II, p. 86)

Wordsworth introduces the poem as follows:

Hart-Leap Well is a small spring of water, about five miles from Richmond in Yorkshire, and near the side of the road that leads from Richmond to Askrigg. Its name is derived from a remarkable Chase, the memory of which is preserved by the monuments spoken of in the second Part of the following Poem, which monuments do now exist as I have there described them.

THE COLUBRIAD: WILLIAM COWPER (II, p. 103)

In a letter, dated 3 August 1782, Cowper gives the following account of this incident:

Passing from the greenhouse to the barn, I saw three kittens... looking with fixed attention at something, which lay on the threshold of a door, coiled up. I took but little notice of them at first; but a loud hiss engaged me to attend more closely, when behold—a viper! the largest I remember to have seen, rearing itself, darting its forked tongue, and ejaculating the afore-mentioned hiss at the nose of a kitten almost in contact with his lips. I ran into the hall for a hoe with a long handle, with which I intended to assail him, and returning in a few seconds missed him: he was gone, and I feared had escaped me. Still, however, the kitten sat watching immoveably upon the same spot. I concluded, therefore, that, sliding between the door and the threshold, he had found his way out of the garden into the yard. I went round immediately, and there found him in close conversation with the old cat, whose curiosity being excited by so novel an appearance, inclined her to pat his head repeatedly with her fore foot; with her claws, however, sheathed, and not in anger; but in the way of philosophical inquiry and examination. To prevent her falling a victim to so laudable an exercise of her talents, I interposed in a moment with the hoe, and performed upon him an act of decapitation, which though not immediately mortal, proved so in the end.

Colubriad, from the Latin word, 'coluber', meaning a snake, is a poetical narrative about a snake, as the Iliad is a poetical narrative about Ilion, or Troy.

A viper, long as Count de Grasse's queue

Count de Grasse was a French admiral who defeated Earl Howe in the West Indies during the War of American Independence. 'Queue' is a hanging plaited tail of hair or wig.

THE PIGEON: RICHARD CHURCH (II, p. 108)

And at the heads of the cables
Stand the serpent-warders

The cables are those attached to the mechanical drills. The serpent-warders are the men who are working these drills, and breaking up the ground with these destroyers ('Thrusting those cruel mouths to their prey').

The image of the drills seen as serpents is continued in the next two lines:

Hark how the steel tongues hiss
As they stab

The steel tongues of the drills (destructive fangs of a serpent) stab the ground. The noise of the drills is 'the clatter that shatters the brain'. The poet writes of this poem: 'The symbolism of the violent and venomous destroyers (the mechanical drills) and the unconscious, feather light creative stamp of the pigeon's feet, is sufficiently clear. It is another version of "the still small voice" that followed the tempest.'

TO A TELEGRAPH POLE: LOUIS UNTERMEYER (II, p. 109)

The telegraph pole is dreaming that it is still a tree with leaves growing closer than the ivy that twines round a bough. The poet says that it should have finished with all thoughts of life ('blossoming') by now. True it was once a tree among others, spruce and pine, not so regularly spaced as they are now. Then the tree was more proud of its branches than of its trunk. This is the last winter that it will be able even to dream. The branches have gone. All that is left is one cross-bar with four rusty strands of wire borne haphazardly. Through these strands of wire ('veins of steel') runs an electric current ('sap') that the tree cannot hope to feel. The birds know that you have no power to feel. They have deceived you. Because they crowd round you as they used to do when you really were alive you think you are still living. The robins in the rain huddled together on the wire strands and those black birds with red shoulders have made you imagine these leaves. These twisting leaves and stems are a final delusion, just as a drowning man clutches at a straw, which he imagines he can see. Do not believe these birds, they are only making fun of you with their warbled song. They know what everyone, except you, knew long ago. The sound of messages humming through your head is not your own. Such sounds along wires make you imagine things. But you are dead.

FACTORY WINDOWS ARE ALWAYS BROKEN: VACHEL LINDSAY (II, p. 110)

Playing ugly Yahoo tricks

In the fourth part of *Gulliver's Travels*, the simplicity and virtues of the Houyhnhnms, horses endowed with reason, are contrasted with the brutality and viciousness of the Yahoos, beasts in the shape of men.

Something is rotten—I think, in Denmark

The comment, 'Something is rotten in the state of Denmark' is made by Marcellus to Horatio after Hamlet followed the beckoning ghost of his murdered father (*Hamlet*, I. iv).

HE WILL WATCH THE HAWK: STEPHEN SPENDER (II, p. 111)

Man who once envied the hawk its power of flight now as the airman will watch it with an indifferent or even a pitiful eye. Man who hunted the eagle till the king of birds was afraid, will now as the airman no more strain his eyes to see this bird. No longer will the airman need to know anything about such antiquated weapons as the stone, the sling and the bow with the tough bow-string. He is now the aristocrat among men. He is splendid in his instinctive reactions in the air. Here, in the presence of death, he has moved at the side of the huge cloud, rising above it he has almost won man's war on the sun. Till now, like Icarus who was drowned in mid-ocean, he, the airman, also crashes into the sea and is drowned; his body ('hands') and his plane ('wings') are found.

Icarus: Daedalus escaped with his son Icarus from Minos, the King of Crete, by making wings. But Icarus, greatly daring, flew too high and the heat of the sun melted the wax by which the wings were fastened to his arms so that he fell in the sea west of Samos, and was drowned.

TO IRON-FOUNDERS AND OTHERS: GORDON BOTTOMLEY
(II, p. 113)

Poison is a key-word of the poem. The apparent exaggeration in the first two lines is corrected in the next two with the statement that no man can live where 'green life', or life-giving vegetation, no longer grows. You, the iron-founders, force the birds to fly too high, that is, above the level or pitch of their natural flight, in their effort to avoid the noxious gases of the iron-foundry. The order of nature is thus disturbed. As a result of this disorder the living rocks, or soil, shall cease to perform a proper function and so they die. You, the iron-founders, have with a thick pall of smoke 'brought down the firmament'. Though this new sky is so much lower than the natural blue sky yet 'no heaven is more near'. 'Heaven' here stands for both the blue heavens above us (now replaced by heavy clouds of smoke) and the happiness which heaven brings. Though you may seem to play with the firmament itself and so give the appearance of performing great deeds these are without importance. Men are now 'half-made', they have lost their innocent belief in heaven and now believe in the power of machines, a belief which also fills them with fear. Now you worship the furnaces of the foundry which have 'molten bowels' just like old idols, huge brazen figures whose worship demanded the obscene practice of human sacrifice. (This recalls the passage in *Paradise Lost*, book I, lines 392–6:

> First Moloch, horrid King besmear'd with blood
> Of human sacrifice, and parents tears,
> Though for the noyse of Drums and Timbrels loud
> Their childrens cries unheard, that past through fire
> To this grim Idol.)

Instead of the beatific vision of the saints, the vision of the iron-founders is of machines for making more machines. Working day and night they are preparing the future of these machines, which is to turn to rust. Such a misuse of iron must have the same effect as poison upon a living creature. The misused iron will be blighted with rust, and then flake and peel away to leave a surface pitted as with a skin disease (tetter'd).

(The Ghost in Hamlet speaks of the effect of poison in these words:

Upon my secure hour thy uncle stole,
With juice of cursed hebenon in a vial,
And in the porches of mine ears did pour
The leperous distilment; whose effect
Holds such an enmity with blood of man,
That, swift as quicksilver, it courses through
The natural gates and alleys of the body;
And, with a sudden vigour, it doth posset
And curd, like eager droppings into milk,
The thin and wholesome blood: so did it mine:
And a most instant tetter bark'd about,
Most lazar-like, with vile and loathsome crust
All my smooth body.)

This dream of machines continues. The grass which was the fore-runner of life has been poisoned, but plants that are able to grow among ruins and broken fragments wait until the dream is done. I have seen hemlock (a poisonous plant) growing in the yards of the iron foundries. But there will be a change. Below the surface of the ground the generations of the worm know nothing about the loads of the machine-age piled on their soil. Their activities will continue, till pushing upwards with the muscular force of nervous energy they make your strong flagstones (replacing the natural soil) heave and stir. The ceaseless activities of the iron-founders, exca-vating the iron-ore, will leave the earth hollow. Then the time will come when the hollowed earth is cracked, and when, to grasp more power and money to spend on feasting, its ores are exhausted, wasted, finished; the rubbish heaps of your burning idols ('beasts') shall be raked over. At last the rubbish heaps will yield the valuable smelting-refuse for the proper tools of mankind: ploughs to turn the soil for grass to grow again in every field, and chisels to increase the skill of men's hands.

TO SOME BUILDERS OF CITIES: STANLEY SNAITH (II, p. 114)

But though you put the Earth in thrall
And ransack all her fragrant dowers

Though you enslave the Earth and plunder all the fragrant gifts of nature.

Her old accomplice, Heaven, will plot
To take with stars your roofs and towers.

Heaven, the old partner of Earth, will plan to capture your roofs and towers with the beauty of the stars.

And neither stone nor steel can foil
That silver strategy of flowers

Buildings made of stone and steel cannot ultimately frustrate the urge of flowers to grow, with their promise of happier times ('silver' suggesting 'silver lining' in Milton's *Comus*).

BELEAGUERED CITIES: F. L. LUCAS (II, p. 115)

Build, build your Babels black against the sky

A reference to the city and the tower which was called Babel (Genesis xi).

Men from your walls shall watch the woods once more
Close round their prey

Cf. *Macbeth:*

Fear not, till Birnam wood
Do come to Dunsinane; and now a wood
Comes toward Dunsinane. (V. v.)

CLOCK: HAROLD MONRO (II, p. 118)

So It, their intimate converging place,
Acquires gigantic intricate communions,
Copious relation to forces beyond forces,
(Cool and placid though it look)

This is a reference to the Theory of Relativity. Einstein maintains that there is no such thing as absolute motion. Motion is always relative to some other object. The laws of nature remain the same only within uniformly moving systems. If, then, absolute motion does not exist, it follows that the idea of absolute time, just as much as absolute space, must be rejected. This is necessary because time and space are related ('copious relation to forces beyond forces'). A year, for example, is measured by the length of time taken for the earth to travel once in its orbit round the sun. A day is the time taken by the earth to make one complete revolution on its axis. If we apply this to the planet Mercury we find a 'year' is only eighty-eight days; since in that time the planet also rotates only once on its axis, a 'year' and a 'day' are the same. Einstein showed that whilst the speed of light is always constant, all measurements of time or space vary according to the velocity of the system within which they are moving.

> *The hidden worlds pursue their time and change;*
> *Are, and then are no more*

This is a reference to the remote galaxies, in which there are some nebulae so many light-years from the earth that light from these 'hidden worlds' may take millions of years to reach us. In fact, it is quite possible that some stars have already ceased to exist ('Are, and then are no more') although their light is still passing through space and we are able to see them in the sky.

> *And visualize the foamy green commotion*
> *Of the great roaring waves that break and fall*

The image of the far-off ocean represents the infinite space in which all the heavenly bodies move. Our knowledge of this is incomplete; we can form in our imagination only some slight conception of the world of space and time.

MATIN SONG: THOMAS HEYWOOD (II, p. 125)

> *Pack, clouds, away! and welcome, day!*

This is an elliptical expression, it means 'Pack up all your possessions, you clouds, and be off!'

> *Bird, prune thy wing!*

'Prune' here means preen, that is, trim your feathers.

AT THE ROUND EARTH'S IMAGINED CORNERS: JOHN DONNE (II, p. 128)

At the four imaginary corners of the round earth blow your trumpets you angels to summon the living and the dead to the last judgement. Arise from the dead you souls without number and without bounds and return to your scattered bodies here upon earth. Prepare for the day of judgement all who were destroyed by the flood and all who will on the last day be destroyed by universal fire; all who have been destroyed by war, famine, old age, fevers, the cruelty of tyrants, despair, the processes of the law and even by chance. And you people who are still alive on the day of judgement and shall not die a mortal death but shall pass directly into everlasting life and behold God face to face, you must prepare yourselves also.

But no, let all these souls sleep, Lord; and let me mourn for a space of time. Because if my sins exceed those of all other men it will be too late to ask for pardon from your abounding goodness when judgement day is actually upon us. Here as I humbly kneel before you teach me how to repent, for if I may repent of my sins that is as good as if you had already sealed my pardon with your blood.

SWEET MUSICK: JOHN FLETCHER (II, p. 130)

Orpheus, a son of the muse Calliope, received from Apollo a lyre (here, a lute) on which he played so skilfully that the wild beasts, rocks, stones and trees came to listen to his song.

THE LOTOS-EATERS: CHORIC SONG: LORD TENNYSON (II, p. 133)

This poem is based on the passage in Homer's *Odyssey*, book IX, which tells how Odysseus and his companions come in their wanderings to the land of the Lotos-eaters on the coast of Africa. Homer describes the effect of the lotos: 'Now whosoever of them did eat the honey-sweet fruit of the lotus, had no more wish to bring tidings nor to come back, but there he chose to abide with the lotos-eating men, ever feeding on the lotos, and forgetful of his homeward way.'

We only toil, who are the first of things

Who are the most important creatures on earth.

'There is no joy but calm!'

The ideal of the Greek philosopher, Epicurus.

Why should we only toil, the roof and crown of things?

The highest of all created things.

In ever climbing up the climbing wave

The repetition of the word 'climbing' suggests the idea of vain effort.

Two handfuls of white dust, shut in an urn of brass!

The Homeric Greeks burned their dead and preserved the ashes in an urn.

Or else the island princes over-bold

The princes on the island of Ithaca wooed Penelope, the wife of Odysseus (Ulysses).

...and the minstrel sings
Before them of the ten years' war in Troy.

In the *Odyssey*, book VIII, Demodocus, the minstrel at the court of Alcinous, sings to Odysseus of the Trojan War.

But, propt on beds of amaranth and moly

Amaranth is the unfading heavenly flower. Moly is the herb given by Hermes to Ulysses to counteract the spells of Circe.

Through many a wov'n acanthus-wreath divine!

Acanthus is a plant with graceful leaves; the shape appears on the capitals of Corinthian columns.

Where the wallowing monster
The whale.

Let us swear an oath, and keep it with an equal mind

Keep it with calmness.

On the hills like Gods together, careless of mankind
A reference to the Gods of Epicurus.

Suffer endless anguish, others in Elysian valleys dwell
The Elysian fields (Elysium): the land of the blest.

Resting weary limbs at last on beds of asphodel
Asphodel is a kind of lily, supposed to cover the Elysian fields.

L'ALLEGRO: JOHN MILTON (II, p. 137)

L'Allegro is Italian for the Cheerful Man. The poem describes the tastes, pleasures and pursuits of the brisk, cheerful man. Milton dismisses Melancholy and calls Mirth (the Nymph) to his side.

Quips and Cranks and wanton Wiles
A quip is 'a short saying of a sharp wit, with a bitter sense in a sweet word'. Cranks are fanciful turns of speech. Wanton wiles are sportive tricks, perhaps practical jokes.

Nods and Becks and wreathèd Smiles
Wreathèd is, here, a transferred epithet. The face is wreathed in smiles.

Such as hang on Hebe's cheek
Hebe was the Greek goddess of Youth, cup-bearer to the gods.

Come, and trip it, as you go
In 'trip it', 'it' is the cognate accusative; perhaps the meaning is 'trip a tripping'. You, Mirth and her companions.

On the light fantastic toe
'Fantastic' means fanciful, as fancy takes you.

The mountain-nymph, sweet Liberty
The mountains are commonly associated with liberty.

To live with her, and live with thee
'Her' refers to Liberty. 'Thee' refers to Mirth.

In unreprovèd pleasures free

Unreprovèd means unreprovable, a Latin use of the participial adjective, common in Elizabethan English.

And, singing, startle the dull night

The lark does sometimes sing just before dawn.

Till the dappled dawn doth rise

'Dappled' here means marked with streaks of light.

Then to come, in spite of sorrow,
And at my window bid good-morrow

These lines are sometimes taken to mean that the lark comes to the poet's window to bid him good-morrow. It is more natural to take 'to come' as parallel in construction to 'to live' and 'to hear', all three verbs depending on 'admit me'. Thus it is the poet who comes to his window and says good morning to the world in general.

'In spite of sorrow' means disdaining sorrow.

Or the twisted eglantine

The epithet 'twisted' suggests that honeysuckle is meant; eglantine and sweet-brier are the same.

Oft list'ning how the hounds and horn

'List'ning' here refers to L'Allegro, the poet.

From the side of some hoar hill

From the side of some hill white with frost.

Sometime walking, not unseen

Not avoiding the public gaze.

Right against the eastern gate
Where the great Sun begins his state

The eastern horizon is regarded as a gateway through which the Sun issues and begins his royal progress ('state').

The clouds in thousand liveries dight

The clouds being decked ('dight') in garments of a thousand different colours.

And every shepherd tells his tale

And every shepherd counts the number (of his sheep). 'Tale' originally meant 'number'.

Straight mine eye hath caught new pleasures

Straightway I see in my mind's eye fresh scenes.

Whilst the landskip round it measures

'Landskip' is landscape, meaning the shape of the land.

Russet lawns, and fallows grey

'Russet' suggests the reddish brown of bracken and fallen leaves, 'lawns' being grasslands, not garden lawns. 'Fallows' are fields left untilled, and so overgrown with grass.

Mountains on whose barren breast

A reference, probably, to the Chiltern Hills.

The labouring clouds do often rest

'Labouring' means in travail, about to bring forth rain; it suggests also the toilsome journey of heavy clouds in need of frequent rest.

Meadows trim with daisies pied

'Pied' means variegated, describing the daisies.

Towers and battlements it sees

'It' refers to 'mine eye'. It is interesting to note that Windsor Castle is visible from Horton in Buckinghamshire where this poem was written.

Bosomed high in tufted trees

Enclosed on a height by clumps of trees.

Where perhaps some beauty lies,
The cynosure of neighbouring eyes

Where some beautiful lady lives, the centre of general attraction. 'Cynosure' is properly the tail (literally, dog's tail) of the Lesser Bear, in which is the pole-star or lode-star.

Where Corydon and Thyrsis met

These are the names of shepherds, as Phillis (properly Phyllis) and Thestylis are names of shepherdesses, in Virgil's *Eclogues*. Milton dignifies the English peasants by using a pastoral convention.

Of herbs and other country messes

Herb gardens were common in Elizabethan times. 'Messes' are savoury dishes.

And then in haste her bower she leaves

A bower is a lady's apartment in a medieval castle.

Or, if the earlier season lead

Or if the hay-harvest call her (Phillis).

To the tanned haycock in the mead

(She goes) to the brown haycock in the meadow.

Sometimes, with secure delight

Delight without a care (Latin 'securus').

And the jocund rebecks sound

The rebeck was a three-stringed fiddle.

And young and old come forth to play

And (the rebecks sound to) young and old who come forth to play.

Then to the spicy nut-brown ale

Shakespeare's 'gossip's bowl' (see *Midsummer Night's Dream*, II. i. 32–57).

With stories told of many a feat

'Feat' means deed (Latin 'factum'). Feat was pronounced fait.

How Faery Mab the junkets eat

Faery Mab was known as the 'fairies' midwife', she was employed to deliver dreams (see *Romeo and Juliet*, I. iv. 54–95). She was fond of cream, hence 'junkets', a dish of sweetened curds and whey with scalded cream on top. 'Eat' is the past tense, ate, and was pronounced 'ate'.

She was pinch'd and pull'd, she said

She, one of the maids, recounting her experiences. The fairies punished sluttish maids by pinching and pulling them. See the ballad, *Robin Goodfellow*:

> When house or hearth doth sluttish lie
> I pinch the maids both black and blue,
> And from the bed the bedcloths I
> Pull off, and lay them nak'd to view.

And he, by Friar's lantern led

And he (one of the youths) said that he was led by a Will o' the Wisp or Jack o' Lantern. The poet seems to have considered Friar Rush (a spirit that haunted houses) the same as 'Friar with the Rush (light)' or Friar with the lantern.

Tells how the drudging goblin sweat
To earn his cream-bowl duly set

Robin Goodfellow, also known as Hobgoblin or Puck, worked at night for households where a bowl of cream was set out for him.

Then lies him down, the lubber fiend

'Lubber fiend' means clownish sprite. Milton may be confusing Puck with a giant called Lob-lie-by-the-fire; though Shakespeare calls Puck 'thou lob of spirits' (*Midsummer Night's Dream*, II. i. 16).

And, stretch'd out all the chimney's length

Stretched out the whole width of the open fire-place.

Basks at the fire his hairy strength

'Basks' is here a transitive verb. 'Hairy strength', his strong hairy body.

And crop-full out of doors he flings

The crop is an enlargement of the gullet in birds, here it is used for stomach, suggesting the animal nature of the goblin.

Ere the first cock his matin rings

Matin is morning prayer. Here, the first crow of the cock at which the fairies and goblins fled.

Tower'd cities please us then

'Then' means after we have considered the pleasures of the countryside.

In weeds of peace, high triumphs hold

Weeds are garments. Triumphs are pageants such as were commonly held at the court of James I.

With store of ladies, whose bright eyes
Rain influence, and judge the prize

'Store' means abundance. 'Influence' originally meant 'the flowing in' of the power of the stars upon the lives of men; here the bright eyes of the ladies, like stars, influence the destinies of men.

Of wit or arms, while both contend
To win her grace whom all commend

'Wit' refers to the then fashionable Courts, or Parliaments of Love—contests in skill of intellect. 'Both' refers to the contests of wit and the contests of arms in which the competition was to win the favour of her (the Queen of the Tournament) whom all commend.

There let Hymen oft appear

Hymen was the god of marriage, a common figure in masques at weddings, where he wore a yellow ('saffron') robe and carried a torch ('taper').

And pomp, and feast, and revelry

'Pomp' is a procession, 'revelry' refers to the court revels which included dancing, music and theatrical shows.

With mask, and antique pageantry

Mask, or masque, was a medley of dance, song, pageantry and dialogue. Pageantry stands for the allegorical shows presented on a stage, often on wheels, and taken on a procession. 'Antique' means 'elaborate', the word was pronounced ántic.

Such sights as youthful poets dream

Milton was twenty-four when he wrote the poem.

Then to the well-trod stage anon

'Well-trod' refers to the quality of plays at this time.

If Jonson's learned sock be on

The *soccus* or slipper was worn at Rome by actors in comedies, the *cothurnus* or high-heeled buskin in tragedies. Ben Jonson was a learned poet, his plays reveal his classical knowledge.

Or sweetest Shakespeare, Fancy's child

Shakespeare is called 'Fancy's child' because his comedies surpass those of Jonson in imagination.

And ever, against eating cares

'Eating cares': gnawing anxieties.

Lap me in soft Lydian airs

The Lydian 'mode' or style of music was tender and voluptuous.

Such as the meeting soul may pierce

'Meeting' means responsive, the soul going out to meet the music.

with many a winding bout

With many an intricate movement.

With wanton heed, and giddy cunning

An example of oxymoron: the use of seeming opposites. With careless care, and dizzy skill.

The melting voice through mazes running,
Untwisting all the chains that tie
The hidden soul of harmony

The sweet voice of music releases the harmony which is lost and bound in every soul.

That Orpheus' self may heave his head

Orpheus, the Thracian poet, went into the infernal regions and so charmed Pluto with his music that Eurydice, his wife, was released from death, on the condition that he would not look back till he reached the Earth. Orpheus looked back on the journey and Eurydice vanished from him for ever.

Milton says that if Orpheus had played music such as this, Pluto would have set Eurydice free without any conditions.

THE LANDSCAPE NEAR AN AERODROME: STEPHEN
SPENDER (II, p. 157)

With burring furred antennae feeling its huge path

'Burring' means with a whirring sound. The spinning propellers
of the air-liner by their position and unsubstantial appearance
suggest the furry antennae of a moth.

Glides over suburbs and the sleeves set trailing tall
To point the wind

The sleeves are wind-socks, canvas cylinders flying from mast-
heads to show the direction of the wind.

Here where industry shows a fraying edge

On the outskirts of the town where industrial buildings are
scattered and untidy.   *the squat buildings*
With their strange air behind trees, like women's faces
Shattered by grief

The low modern buildings, out of harmony with the trees surrounding them, have a lifeless air, like women's faces lacking beauty
and vivacity.   *Here where few houses*
Moan with faint light behind their blinds
They remark the unhomely sense of complaint

They (the travellers in the air-liner) notice the isolation of a few
houses which seem to express their sad loneliness ('moan') by the
dim glow of the lights behind the drawn blinds. (The essential
loneliness of the human spirit.)

In the last sweep of love

As though the air-liner is wooing the 'feminine' land.

Then, as they land, they hear the tolling bell
Reaching across the landscape of hysteria

From the air-liner the land looked beautiful; now, as the plane
touches down the passengers hear the church bell sounding across
the landscape marred by modern industry, 'the charcoaled batteries'
and 'imaged towers'.

Religion stands, the church blocking the sun

The achievements of modern invention may lead man to think he is self-sufficient. The poet reminds us that religion, still part of the modern scene, is more important ('larger than all the charcoaled batteries').

THE PYLONS: STEPHEN SPENDER (II, p. 158)

The first three verses of this poem express the contrast between the natural and the unnatural. When stone was quarried from the hills they yielded up their secret. Cottages, roads and villages were made of this stone, a 'natural' product. Now, over these hills they have built concrete pylons; these pillars are 'unnatural'. The valley with its golden haze in the evening; the chestnut tree with its 'customary' (or natural) root are now mocked by the advent of the pylons which bring with them a new age.

> *But far above and far as sight endures*
> *Like whips of anger*
> *With lightning's danger*
> *There runs the quick perspective of the future*

But the electric cable ('the quick perspective of the future') carried by the pylons runs high above us and as far as the eye can see like the cracking sound of whips flicked in anger and with the danger of lightning in its high voltage.

> *This dwarfs our emerald country by its trek*
> *So tall with prophecy*

This, the electric cable, so clearly foretelling the great changes in the future, makes our green country seem small by its journey ('far above and far as sight endures').

> *Dreaming of cities*
> *Where often clouds shall lean their swan-white neck*

The electric cable dreams of cities built of steel and concrete so tall that the clouds shall rest upon them.

14-2

CRUCIFIXION OF THE SKYSCRAPER: J. GOULD FLETCHER
(II, p. 159)

The building of the skyscraper is described in a way that recalls the crucifixion of Christ who was nailed on the Cross ('nailed it to the rock'); suffered physical agony ('each nerve and vein searched by iron hammers'); was placed in a sepulchre, which was our 'tomb of hope'; guarded by His followers ('throngs of acolytes'); and finally rose to realms of light ('the skyscraper dripped light').

> *Within its walls*
> *Men laid a little gold*

may refer to the filaments of the electric lights which at night produce the transformation:

> *Lone on the velvety night in flights of gold*
> *The tower rose.*

THE LADY OF SHALOTT: LORD TENNYSON (II, p. 184)

This poem is based upon an Italian story, *Donna di Scalotta*. Shalott is the anglicized form of Scalotta.

> *That clothe the wold and meet the sky*

Wold: weald, downs.

> *To many-tower'd Camelot*

Camelot was King Arthur's legendary capital.

> *Willows whiten, aspens quiver*

The willows would whiten by showing the underside of the leaf.

> *The shallop flitteth silken-sail'd*

A shallop is a light open boat. It is 'unhail'd', that is, no one calls out to it.

> *A magic web with colours gay*

A tapestry with bright-coloured threads.

> *She knows not what the curse may be*

The curse that falls on her is that of unrequited love.

An abbot on an ambling pad
On a slowly pacing pony.

Of bold Sir Lancelot
Lancelot was the most famous of the Knights of the Round Table.

Hung in the golden Galaxy
The golden Galaxy is the Milky Way.

And from his blazon'd baldric slung
A baldric is a belt, here ornamented with heraldic devices.

Some bearded meteor, trailing light
Some shooting-star with light like a beard trailing behind it.

THE BLESSÈD DAMOZEL: DANTE GABRIEL ROSSETTI
(II, p. 190)
Damozel: a damsel, a maiden of noble birth.

She had three lilies in her hand
Pythagoras calls three the perfect number.

And the stars in her hair were seven
Seven is the holy or mystic number.

Her robe, ungirt from clasp to hem
It was the fashion of nuns to wear a robe without a girdle from the neck ('clasp') to hem.

But a white rose of Mary's gift
The rose was a symbol of the Virgin Mary.

Herseemed she scarce had been a day
It seemed to her that she had scarcely been one day.

Albeit, to them she left, her day...
Although to those people she had left on Earth, her day....

(To one, it is ten years of years.)

To the man who loved her, the day is as long as ten years each year consisting of 365 years instead of 365 days.

Nothing: the autumn fall of leaves

'This was merely my imagination; it was only the falling leaves of autumn that touched my face.'

It was the rampart of God's house

In the Middle Ages Heaven was thought of as a castle and would have ramparts on top of the walls.

Time like a pulse shake fierce
Through all the worlds

Time throbbing rhythmically through all the worlds in space.

Her voice was like the voice the stars
Had when they sang together

A reference to the stars singing together at the creation of the world. 'When the morning stars sang together, And all the sons of God shouted for joy' (Job xxxviii).

Are not two prayers a perfect strength?
And shall I feel afraid?

A probable reference to the following words in St Matthew: 'Again I say unto you, that if two of you shall agree on earth as touching anything that they shall ask, it shall be done for them of my Father which is in heaven.'

When round his head the aureole clings

The aureole was the circle of light round the head of angels. Here, when he is an angel in heaven.

To the deep wells of light

Revelation xxii. i: 'And he shewed me a river of water of life, bright as crystal, proceeding out of the throne of God.'

We two will stand beside that shrine

Here, the holy sanctuary of Heaven.

Occult, withheld, untrod

Kept secret, withheld, unapproachable. The shrine is not for the uninitiated.

Whose lamps are stirred continually
With prayer sent up to God

Revelation iv. 5: 'And there were seven lamps of fire burning before the throne, which are the seven Spirits of God.'

And see our old prayers, granted, melt
Each like a little cloud

Revelation v. 8: 'And when he had taken the book, the four living creatures and the four and twenty elders fell down before the Lamb, having each one a harp, and golden bowls full of incense, which are the prayers of the saints.'

We two will lie i' the shadow of
That living mystic tree

Revelation xxii. 2: 'And on this side of the river and on that was the tree of life, bearing twelve manner of fruits, yielding its fruit every month.'

Within whose secret growth the Dove

Here the Dove is the Holy Spirit.

'Circle-wise sit they, with bound locks
And foreheads garlanded'

They sit in a circle with their hair tied up, and with garlands round their heads.

Who are just born, being dead

Who are born into Heaven, having died on Earth.

To their citherns and citoles

These are wire-stringed, lute-like instruments usually played with plectrum.

EVE: RALPH HODGSON (II, p. 196)

Humble proud heaven

Satan, here the cobra, had led a rebellion in heaven and had been defeated. Now he was seeking his revenge ('to get even') by causing the downfall of man, whom God had created and placed in the Garden of Eden.

The Blasphemous Tree

This is the tree of the knowledge of good and evil which grew in the Garden of Eden. For man to acquire this knowledge is a kind of blasphemy against God.

GOBLIN MARKET: CHRISTINA ROSSETTI (II, p. 198)

W. M. Rossetti writes of this poem in his Notes to Christina Rossetti's *Poems* as follows:

In this narrative the goblins tempt women to eat their luscious but uncanny fruits; a first taste produces a rabid craving for a second taste; but the second taste is never accorded, and, in default of it, the woman pines away and dies. Laura having tasted the fruits once, and being at death's door through inability to get a second taste, her sister Lizzie determines to save her at all hazards; so she goes to the goblins, refuses to eat their fruits, and beguiles them into forcing the fruits upon her with so much insistency that her face is all smeared and steeped with the juices; she gets Laura to kiss and suck these juices off her face, and Laura, having thus obtained the otherwise impossible second taste, rapidly recovers.

Apples and quinces

A quince is a hard, acid, yellowish, pear-shaped fruit used for flavouring.

Dates and sharp bullaces

A bullace is a small wild plum, like a damson.

One like a wombat prowled obtuse and furry,
One like a ratel tumbled hurry skurry

A wombat is a small Australian bear. A ratel is the South African honey-badger.

216

Must she no more such succous pasture find

'Succous' means the same as succulent or juicy.

That juice was wormwood to her tongue

Wormwood is a herb with a bitter taste; here it means bitter.

And win the fiery antidote

And win the counteracting medicine which tasted bitter to her (Laura), or was obtained at such painful cost.

THE FORSAKEN MERMAN: MATTHEW ARNOLD (II, p. 214)

This poem may very well be based upon the following Danish legend which was related by George Borrow as follows:

There lived once two poor people near Friesenborg, in the district of Aarhuus in Jutland, who had one only child, a daughter, called Grethe. One day that they sent her down to the sea-shore to fetch some sand, as she was washing her apron, a merman arose out of the water. His beard was greener than the salt sea; his shape was pleasing, and he spoke to the girl in a kind and friendly tone, and said, 'Come with me, Grethe, and I will give you as much gold and silver as your heart can wish.' 'That were not badly done', replied she, 'for we have very little of it at home.' She let herself be prevailed on, and he took her by the hand, and brought her down to the bottom of the sea, and she in course of time became the mother of five children. When a long time had passed over, and she had nearly forgotten all she knew of religion, one festival morning as she was sitting with her youngest child in her lap, she heard the church bells ringing above, and there came over her mind great uneasiness, and anxious longing to go to church. And as she sat there with her children, and sighed heavily, the merman observed her affliction, and enquired what made her so melancholy. She then coaxed him, and earnestly entreated him to let her go once more to church. The merman could not withstand her tears and solicitations, so he set her on the land, and charged her strictly to make haste back to the children. In the middle of the sermon, the merman came to the outside of the church, and cried 'Grethe! Grethe! will you come quick? your children are crying for you.' But when she did not come, he began to weep bitterly, and went back to the bottom of the sea. But Grethe ever after stayed with her parents, and let the merman himself take care of his ugly little children, and his weeping and lamentation have often been heard from the bottom of the deep.

In Matthew Arnold's poem the merman is speaking. He is telling his children how Margaret, his mortal wife, has returned to her old home in the white-walled town beside the sea.

The poem has a deeper significance. The kingdom under the sea where the merman lives represents the old pagan world of Greek mythology with its beauty and sense of wonder. Arnold profoundly regrets its passing in favour of the grey joylessness of organized religion. He refers to this when Margaret returns to the town and the 'little grey church on the windy shore'.

A similar feeling of regret for the loss of the sense of values of the ancient world is expressed by Wordsworth in this sonnet:

> *The world is too much with us; late and soon,*
> *Getting and spending, we lay waste our powers;*
> *Little we see in Nature that is ours;*
> *We have given our hearts away, a sordid boon!*
> *This sea that bares her bosom to the moon;*
> *The winds that will be howling at all hours,*
> *And are up-gathered now like sleeping flowers;*
> *For this, for everything, we are out of tune;*
> *It moves us not.—Great God! I'd rather be*
> *A Pagan suckled in a creed outworn;*
> *So might I, standing on this pleasant lea,*
> *Have glimpses that would make me less forlorn;*
> *Have sight of Proteus rising from the sea;*
> *Or hear old Triton blow his wreathèd horn.*

OUTLAWS: ROBERT GRAVES (II, p. 224)

This poem contrasts the power of the old gods in the past, when as Zeus, Jupiter, Thor, Odin, they spoke 'with thunder from an open sky', and the mere superstition of today which peoples the dark wood with 'bogey things'. As long as superstitious fears remain these aged gods will 'cling to life yet' though fallen from their high estate.

THE PERFECT LIFE: BEN JONSON (II, p. 228)

These lines are part of an ode 'To the Immortal Memory and Friendship of that Noble Pair, Sir Lucius Cary and Sir Henry Morison'. Sir Lucius Cary (later Lord Falkland) was killed at the first battle of Newbury in 1643.

The theme is simple: that quality is better than quantity.

> *Or standing long an oak, three hundred year,*
> *To fall a log at last, dry, bald, and sere*

Or standing for a long time, say, three hundred years, to fall a log at last, dry, bald and withered that does not make an oak better.

> *Is fairer far in May*

A lily is much fairer than an oak, even in May when the oak is at its best.

> *It was the plant and flower of Light*

In Christian art the lily is an emblem of purity.

> *In small proportions we just beauties see*

'Just' is here a Latinism for 'perfect'.

SWEET CONTENT: THOMAS DEKKER (II, p. 228)

This poem has been called 'the golden hymn of contentment'.

> *Art thou poor, yet hast thou golden slumbers?*

'Golden', a most evocative word, here means delightful.

> *To add to golden numbers golden numbers?*

Golden numbers here means gold coins.

> *Canst drink the waters of the crispèd spring?*

'Crispèd' here means rippling. (Latin 'crispus', curled.)

No burden bears, but is a king, a king!

A reference to the belief of the Stoic philosophers that 'a wise man alone is free, and not only free, but even a king'.

THE CHARACTER OF A HAPPY LIFE: SIR HENRY WOTTON
(II, p. 229)

How happy is he born and taught
That serveth not another's will

How happy is the man who by natural disposition and by training does not serve another man.

Whose soul is still prepared for death

Whose soul is always prepared for death.

Untied unto the world by care
Of public fame or private breath

Who is not tied to the world by anxiety of winning popular approval or the favour of influential patrons ('private breath').

Who envies none whom chance doth raise
Nor vice

Who envies no one who has been successful in life through good fortune or through dishonesty.

who never understood
How deepest wounds are given by praise

By hypocritical praise given in order to excite the jealousy and enmity of others.

Nor rules of state, but rules of good

(Who envies no one who succeeds) by the tricks of the politician rather than by personal integrity.

Who hath his life from rumours freed

Who cannot be harmed by gossip.

Whose state can neither flatterers feed

'State' here means 'estate', hence 'wealth'.

Nor ruin make oppressors great

'Ruin' means downfall. Who is not so wealthy that a tyrant (or oppressor) would profit by his downfall and the confiscation of his property. (In Roman times a successful accuser received one-fourth of the condemned man's estate.)

Who God doth late and early pray
More of His grace than gifts to lend

Who prays to God early and late to give him more of His blessing than to bestow gifts upon him.

And entertains the harmless day

'Entertains' means passes agreeably.

—This man is freed from servile bands
Of hope to rise or fear to fall

This man is freed from the enslaving bonds of ambition or fear of failure.

INTEGER VITAE: THOMAS CAMPION (II, p. 229)

See Horace *Integer vitae* (Odes, I. 22)

Nor sorrow discontent

Nor sorrow make discontented. (The verb is now confined to the past participle.)

The earth his sober inn

Compare the passage in Cicero's *De Senectute*: 'I part from life as from an inn, not from my home; for Nature has given it to us as a hostelry wherein to sojourn, not as a place to dwell in.'

DEATH THE LEVELLER: JAMES SHIRLEY (II, p. 232)

The glories of our mortal condition (including both nobility and position in the world of affairs) are only shadows, not solid possessions. There is no defence against Fate. Death comes to kings, they must die just as farm labourers ('poor crookèd scythe and spade') must die. Some men with swords may gain new glory by killing the enemy in the field of battle. But their strong muscles must yield at last. Soldiers tame only one another always, they do not tame Fate. They must inevitably, early or late stoop to Fate, giving up their protesting breath when they creep to death as pale captives. The garlands ('wreaths of the victor') wither then on your head. Therefore you have no cause to boast of your mighty victories. Look where the victor, now a victim, bleeds upon the blood-stained altar of Death. You must all come to the cold tomb. Only the actions of those who have been just upon earth will smell sweet and blossom in their own dust in the tomb.

VIRTUE: GEORGE HERBERT (II, p. 233)

Sweet rose, whose hue, angry and brave

Sweet rose whose colour is red as with anger and resplendent or bright.

A box where sweets compacted lie

A box where sweet things lie closely pressed together.

My music shows ye have your closes

The music of my verse shows that the beauties of spring must come to an end like the cadences or conclusions of musical phrases. The last verse means that although the day, the rose and spring must all die, only a sweet and virtuous soul like seasoned timber never gives way or breaks, and even though the whole world should turn to coal, that is, become fuel at the day of judgement, then the soul will certainly live.

ON THE TOMBS IN WESTMINSTER ABBEY: FRANCIS BEAUMONT (II, p. 233)

Mortality, behold and fear!

You mortals, behold what a change of flesh is here and be filled with fear!

Sleep within this heap of stones

Either in these tombs, or in this abbey.

Here they lie had realms and lands

Here they lie who had realms and lands.

Where from their pulpits seal'd with dust

The 'pulpits' are the tombs in which they lie. 'Seal'd' means closed in. *They preach, 'In greatness is no trust.'*

See Psalm 146. 3: 'O put not your trust in princes, nor in any child of man: for there is no help in them.'

Here's an acre sown indeed

The metaphor of the acre is continued in the words 'sown' and 'seed' (compare: God's acre).

Here the bones of birth have cried—

Here the bones of men of noble birth have cried—.

Here are sands, ignoble things

'Sands' are the ashes of dissolution.

Buried in dust, once dead by fate

'Once dead' means dead once for all.

ELEGY WRITTEN IN A COUNTRY CHURCHYARD: THOMAS
GRAY (II, p. 234)

R. W. Ketton-Cremer says of the *Elegy*:

It is almost impossible to analyse a work which for two centuries has formed a part of the English heritage, so familiar, so constantly quoted, so universally beloved. The exquisite twilight scene with which it opens; the long series of reflections upon fame and obscurity, ambition and destiny; those stanzas, tolling like solemn bells, which seem to voice all that can be expressed of sadness, resignation and hope—since childhood they have been a part of our consciousness, exerting upon us the same irresistible spell as they did upon our forefathers. For all its familiarity the *Elegy* retains to an extraordinary degree its original eloquence and mystery, its power to move the heart with those 'divine truisms that make us weep'.

Parts of the poem do, however, present some difficulty and need, perhaps, brief explanation.

The Curfew tolls the knell of parting day

The evening bell was still conventionally called curfew, though the law of William the Conqueror which gave it the name had long been a dead letter.

The lowing herd wind slowly o'er the lea

The word 'wind' has a poetical connotation, for it suggests a long slowly moving line of cattle rather than a herd closely packed.

And all the air a solemn stillness holds

'Stillness' is the subject and 'air' is the object. A solemn stillness holds all the air captive.

The rude Forefathers of the hamlet sleep

'Rude' means simple, unlettered. The poor people were buried in the churchyard; the rich inside the church.

No more shall rouse them from their lowly bed

'Lowly bed' probably refers to the humble bed in which they spent the night, but it is meant to suggest the grave as well.

Or busy housewife ply her evening care

Here 'care' means task.

Their furrow oft the stubborn glebe has broke

'Glebe' means ploughland (more exactly, land going with a clergyman's benefice).

How jocund did they drive their team afield!

How cheerfully they drove their team to the field.

Let not Ambition mock their useful toil

Do not let ambitious people speak contemptuously of their useful labours.

Nor Grandeur hear with a disdainful smile
The short and simple annals of the poor

Do not let people of high position hear with a pitying smile the short and simple accounts of the doings of the poor.

> *The boast of heraldry, the pomp of pow'r,*
> *And all that beauty, all that wealth e'er gave,*
> *Awaits alike th' inevitable hour*

'Hour' is here the nominative. The inevitable hour, that is, death, waits for proud people of noble ancestry, for those who hold positions of power in public life, for those who are beautiful and those who are wealthy.

> *Can storied urn or animated bust*
> *Back to its mansion call the fleeting breath?*

Can an urn with a story or inscription on it (a common form of funeral monument in imitation, more or less, of the antique), or a bust so realistic that it seemed that life had been breathed into it, bring back life to the dead body (mansion)?

> *Can Honour's voice provoke the silent dust,*
> *Or Flatt'ry soothe the dull cold ear of Death?*

'Provoke' means call to life, rouse to action; 'soothe' means to humour and so persuade or win over.

> *Some heart once pregnant with celestial fire*

Some person full of divine inspiration.

> *Hands, that the rod of empire might have sway'd,*
> *Or wak'd to ecstasy the living lyre*

Some person who might have become a great ruler, or an inspired poet.

> *Chill Penury repress'd their noble rage,*
> *And froze the genial current of the soul*

Restricting poverty stopped their ardent ambition, and checked the fervour and creative power of genius.

> *Some village-Hampden that with dauntless breast*

Hampden was a Buckinghamshire squire, M.P. for Wendover and cousin to Cromwell.

> *Some mute inglorious Milton here may rest*

Some man who might have become a great poet.

> *Some Cromwell guiltless of his country's blood*

Some man with the qualities of leadership who might not have plunged his country into civil war.

Th' applause of list'ning senates to command

To command the applause of legislative assemblies.

Their lot forbade: nor circumscribed alone
Their growing virtues, but their crimes confined

Their obscure lot prevented them not only from developing their good qualities but also from committing crimes.

The struggling pangs of conscious truth to hide,
To quench the blushes of ingenuous shame,
Or heap the shrine of Luxury and Pride
With incense kindled at the Muse's flame

Their obscure lot also prevented them from becoming unscrupulous place-hunters given to lying and hypocrisy, or from becoming courtly and venal poets ('at the Muse's flame') flattering those who live a life of luxury and outward display.

They kept the noiseless tenor of their way

They continued the uneventful course of their lives.

Their name, their years, spelt by th' unletter'd muse,
The place of fame and elegy supply:
And many a holy text around she strews,
That teach the rustic moralist to die

The rough tombstones of the poor with their misspelt inscriptions giving name and age take the place of the eloquent monuments of the famous; and she ('th' unletter'd muse') inscribes many a text from the Bible that teaches the thoughtful rustic how to become reconciled to death.

For who, to dumb Forgetfulness a prey,
This pleasing anxious being e'er resign'd,
Left the warm precincts of the cheerful day,
Nor cast one longing ling'ring look behind?

At this point in the poem a fresh note begins to be heard, 'a sudden note of human loneliness and anguish in the face of death'. The poet asks what person being a prey to silent reverie ever resigned himself, a mixture of pleasant sensations and acute anxieties, to death, leaving this warm, familiar world without casting one last look of longing behind him?

> *On some fond breast the parting soul relies,*
> *Some pious drops the closing eye requires*

When a man is dying he relies upon the ministrations of a friend, and he wants to know that devout tears will be shed upon his death.

In the next stanza Gray becomes the central figure of the poem and remains so till the end. He is thinking of himself as the author of 'these lines' that tell the story of 'th' unhonour'd dead'. Then he imagines 'some hoary-headed Swain', an old countryman, telling 'some kindred spirit', a passer-by, of the fate of the poet ('thy fate'). Then follows a strangely dramatized description of the poet (as seen by the old countryman) telling of his wanderings, of how he would rest at the foot of a beech tree and watch the brook flowing by, and finally, of his untimely death. The dead poet is buried in the churchyard with those humble and obscure people whose 'artless tale' he has related.

The last three stanzas form Gray's epitaph upon himself. They may seem a little fanciful, on the other hand they may as R. W. Ketton-Cremer says 'describe simply and movingly what sort of man Gray believed himself to be, how he fared in his passage through the world, and what he hoped from eternity'.

PATCH-SHANEEN: J. M. SYNGE (II, p. 238)

> *Lived west in Carnareagh*

A village in County Kerry.

> *She'd pick her bag of carrageen*
> *Or perries through the surf*

Carrageen is an edible sea-weed, sometimes known as Irish moss. Perries are pebbles; more usually, precious stones.

> *To fetch her creel of turf*

To fetch a large wicker basket filled with peat.

Till on one windy Samhain night

The Celtic year ended on October 31st, the eve of Samhain (Halloween). For the Druids in pre-Christian Ireland, Samhain was both the 'end of summer' and a festival of the dead. The spirits of the dead ('there's stir among the dead') were believed to visit their kinsmen in search of warmth and comfort as winter approached.

Beside the seed of fire

Beside the tiniest flicker of fire.

PROGNOSIS: LOUIS MACNEICE (II, p. 243)

Prognosis: the foretelling of events.

The poem consists of a series of questions asking what the future may bring. The future is regarded as a stranger coming in a variety of different forms. The future, then, may bring increased opportunities in business, or personal happiness. It may bring its own problems which have to be solved. The future may bring something quite unexpected like a pedlar with his pack containing things one does not want ('he comes to beg') or greatly desires ('he comes to bargain'). Will the future offer all kinds of opportunities with promises of success, or will circumstances be harshly restricted? Will it offer the assurances of John the apostle, or be the bearer of ill-luck like Jonah. (Iona or Icolmkill is an island of the Inner Hebrides where St Columba founded a monastery in 563 and called upon the Picts to repent.) Will it call to an adventurous life as Jason summoned the heroes who sailed with him on board the 'Argo' to Colchis to recover the Golden Fleece? Or will it offer some futile activity? (For two centuries between 1095 and 1271 there were eight crusades in all; millions of lives and an enormous amount of treasure were sacrificed in these enterprises, and when all was done Jerusalem remained in the possession of the 'infidels'.) What will its message be—war or work or marriage? Will it bring some news that is really new, or only some old traditional maxim? Will the future answer my probing question, or will it avoid any clear explanation? Will love be the name of the future and its message be beyond our understanding, or will its name be Death whose message is so easy to accept?

THE CHARIOT: EMILY DICKINSON (II, p. 245)

We are reminded, if by way of contrast, of the story of Elijah, II Kings ii. 11: 'And it came to pass, as they still went on, and talked, that, behold, there appeared a chariot of fire, and horses of fire, which parted them both asunder; and Elijah went up by a whirlwind into heaven.'

> *The roof was scarcely visible,*
> *The cornice but a mound*

A grave consisting of a mound of earth. A cornice is a horizontal moulded projection crowning a building.

PEACE: HENRY VAUGHAN (II, p. 246)

> *Leave then thy foolish ranges*

'Ranges' means wanderings.

> *Thy God, thy life, thy cure*

'Cure' here means salvation.

AND DEATH SHALL HAVE NO DOMINION: DYLAN THOMAS (II, p. 246)

The theme of the poem is that man cannot be annihilated by death because of his immortal soul.

> *Dead men naked they shall be one*
> *With the man in the wind and the west moon*

The bodies of dead men shall be as real as the 'man in the wind' and the 'west moon', that is no longer real at all.

When their bones are picked clean and the clean bones gone

This line recalls the drowned Phoenician Sailor in *The Waste Land*:

> *A current under sea*
> *Picked his bones in whispers.*

This death by water would seem to suggest the death described in Ariel's song in *The Tempest*:

> *Full fathom five thy father lies;*
> *Of his bones are coral made.*

They shall have stars at elbow and foot

They (the dead men) shall be translated to another sphere just as mythological figures such as Hercules, Perseus, Orion, live again as constellations in the heavens, 'with stars at elbow and foot'.

Though they go mad they shall be sane

Though men go mad on earth they shall regain sanity in the world of the spirit.

Though they sink through the earth they shall rise again

Though they descend into hell, the place of the dead, they shall rise again.

Under the windings of the sea
They lying long shall not die windily

Though they, the dead men, may be lying for a long time in the winding currents of the sea yet they shall not die full of fear ('windily').

Twisting on racks when sinews give way
Strapped to a wheel, yet they shall not break

The most notorious instruments of torture were the rack and the wheel. Even under torture the spirit of man shall triumph.

Faith in their hands shall snap in two

Even though their belief in God shall (under torture) snap like a stick yet they shall survive in spirit.

230

And the unicorn evil runs them through

The unicorn, a fabulous beast, was thought of in mediaeval times as possessing great strength and fierceness. Here it symbolizes evil. Though men may be destroyed by evil yet they shall be saved by the spirit.

Split all ends up they shall not crack

The image of violent torture is continued. Though the bodies of men are split (like the trunks of trees) yet they shall not be destroyed in spirit.

No more may gulls cry at their ears
Or waves break loud on the seashores

The dead men shall no longer hear the cry of the sea-gulls, or the sound of breaking waves; common sounds on Earth.

Where blew a flower may a flower no more
Lift its head to the blows of the rain

The dead men shall no longer see the violence of nature, the flower beaten down by heavy rain.

Though they be mad and as dead as nails
Heads of the characters hammer through daisies

Though the dead men may have been mad on earth and are now apparently quite dead, yet just as the life-force makes the daisies, so the human spirit is made to survive. The imagery in the second line above is of the distinctive mark impressed as an image ('heads') upon a coin to make it recognizable, so the distinguishing mark of a species of flower is forced ('hammer') though the mystery of growth to become daisies.

Break in the sun till the sun breaks down,
And death shall have no dominion

Man can suffer and die on this earth ('in the sun') till the sun itself is extinguished, and yet death shall not annihilate man's immortal spirit.

231

BOOK LIST

The following books are suggested for further reading:

NORMAN CALLAN, *Poetry in Practice* (Lindsay Drummond).

W. EMPSON, *Seven Types of Ambiguity* (Chatto and Windus).

A. E. HOUSMAN, *The Name and Nature of Poetry* (Cambridge University Press).

F. R. LEAVIS, *New Bearings in English Poetry* (Chatto and Windus).

C. DAY LEWIS, *A Hope for Poetry* (Blackwell).

——, *The Poetic Image* (Cape).

P. H. B. LYON, *The Discovery of Poetry* (Arnold).

LOUIS MACNEICE, *Modern Poetry* (Oxford University Press).

I. A. RICHARDS, *Principles of Literary Criticism* (Kegan Paul).

——, *Practical Criticism* (Kegan Paul).

M. R. RIDLEY, *Poetry and the Ordinary Reader* (Bell).

STEPHEN SPENDER, *The Destructive Element* (Cape).

E. M. W. TILLYARD, *Poetry Direct and Oblique* (Chatto and Windus).

MARTIN TURNELL, *Poetry and Crisis* (Sands).